THAT OTHERS MIGHT LIVE

THAT OTHERS

MIGHT LIVE

The U.S. Life-Saving Service, 1878–1915

Dennis L. Noble

NAVAL INSTITUTE PRESS
Annapolis, Maryland

Library of Congress Cataloging-in-Publication Data
Noble, Dennis L.
That others might live : the U.S. Life-Saving Service, 1878–1915 / Dennis L. Noble.
p. cm.
Includes bibliographical references and index.
ISBN 1-55750-627-2
1. United States. Life-Saving Service—History. 2. Life-saving—United States—History. I. Title.
VK1323.N63 1994
363.12′381′0973—dc20 93-37539

Printed in the United States of America on acid-free paper ♾

9 8 7 6 5 4 3 2
First printing

This book is for my mother
and to the memory of my father.

These poor, plain men, dwellers upon the lonely sands of Hatteras, took their lives in their hands, and, at the most imminent risk, crossed the most tumultuous sea . . . , and all for what? That others might live to see home and friends.

— *Annual Report of the Operations of the United States Life-Saving Service, 1885*

Contents

Preface

Many years ago, when I was a young "boot" in the U.S. Coast Guard, my first duty station was at a unit that originally had been under the U.S. Life-Saving Service. The duty was sometimes arduous, sometimes extremely boring, but one could never tell when it would become dangerous. One member of the station won the Gold Life Saving Medal during my tour of duty. I felt then, as I do now, that the humanitarian aspect of the U.S. Coast Guard is the essence of the service. As I began to delve into the history of the U.S. Coast Guard, I found that the service's predecessors have been largely overlooked. Yet one, the U.S. Life-Saving Service, is the foundation upon which the U.S. Coast Guard's reputation in rescue rests. I came to marvel at the accomplishments of the lifesavers. I can recall hanging onto a pitching and rolling motor lifeboat, with waves breaking over us, and wondering what in the hell I had gotten myself into. This, however, was nothing compared to what the crews of the U.S. Life-Saving Service endured when they pushed out into howling gales and heavy seas in small pulling boats. If this book can shed light on these early lifesavers and bring about a recognition of their efforts, then it will have served its purpose.

Why did an organization so obviously based on humanitarian efforts slip behind the veil of time? Besides detailing the lives of the lifesavers, their equipment, and rescues, this book explores the reasons behind the scant amount of information on the service. One reason for this lack of knowledge is that no books have been written about the U.S. Life-Saving Service as a national entity. A number of books either have the service in the title or begin by mentioning the service, but the authors become fascinated with wrecks and rescues and do not explore the service or do so only superficially. This is understandable; the rescues and shipwrecks are exciting. Some books deal with the service in more detail, but these are usually limited to individual stations or regions, such as the Great Lakes or the Outer Banks of North Carolina. I am not implying that such books are not useful. Indeed, good, documented histories on each station, such as Edward J. Canfield and Thomas A. Allan's *Life on a Lonely Shore: A History of the Vermilion Point Life-Saving Station* (1991), are needed for a complete picture of the U.S. Life-Saving Service.

The official in charge of a unit, the keeper, had a great deal of autonomy. If he could pass periodic inspections, he had all the freedom of a nineteenth-century ship captain. Therefore, a history that reflects the U.S. Life-Saving Service as a national organization will, at times, be at odds with what was happening at some units. This book reflects a national organization, based on the published regulations of the service. I encourage historians and local and state historical societies to produce documented books and articles on the individual stations in their areas. When these stations are properly recorded, the rich legacy of this aspect of maritime history will be better appreciated.

Many of the books dealing with the service become sidetracked by the excitement of rescues. I would be remiss in any account of the U.S. Life-Saving Service if I did not include some rescues. After all, this was the raison d'être for the organization. Indeed, one of the most difficult tasks in writing this book was deciding what rescues to include—not because of a lack of documentation, but because of the abundance of cases from which to choose. Few historians can complain that they have too much material to work with, but this is the case when it comes to wrecks and rescues. If only those rescues for which crewmen won the Gold Life Saving medal—the highest award offered by the service—were included this book would be very long. My principal criterion for selecting rescues was simple: Does the rescue illustrate a point being stressed in the narrative? A secondary criterion was to select rescues from as many regions as possible to reflect the national scope of the organization. One could easily fill a book twice this size with the rescues that occurred only along the Outer Banks. A few regions have not been represented, or have been represented very thinly, but to cover every wreck is impossible and this book deals with the service as a national entity. Whenever possible I have used the language of the contemporary press, reports, and witnesses. Although some of the language may border on purple prose, I believe it will help the modern reader understand why the reading public of that day thought of the lifesavers as "storm warriors."

Chapter 2 discusses the events leading up to the formation of the U.S. Life-Saving Service. Robert F. Bennett and Dennis R. Means have covered this period so thoroughly that I felt it was necessary to provide only an overview of this era. And the emphasis of this book is on the U.S. Life-Saving Service beginning in 1878 and ending in 1915. Chapter 3 deals largely with the administrative background of the service; chapter 4 offers some insight into who made up the crews of the organization. To provide an understanding of the actual rescues of the service, chapters 5 and 6 deal with the principal tools of the lifesavers: boats and beach apparatus. Chapter 7 offers some insight into life at a station and chapter 8 deals with the ending of the service. The views expressed within this book are mine.

Acknowledgments

Over the years I have visited with many people in search of information on the U.S. Life-Saving Service (USLSS). I thank all who have put up with my questions and requests. I would be remiss, however, not to especially thank those who have helped in the preparation of this book.

William Sherman, at the National Archives, has made available the primary sources needed to write this work. Since my first request to him, some eighteen years ago, he has always promptly handled my inquiries and found even the most obscure record. Teresa Matchett, during her tenure in the same division of the National Archives, was also very helpful. Richard H. Smith, of the Cartographic and Architectural Branch of the National Archives, helped greatly in locating drawings of stations.

Dr. Robert M. Browning, historian of the U.S. Coast Guard, has gone above and beyond the call of duty in responding to my many requests for photographs and other information. Despite operating with only a small staff, he always cheerfully and quickly sent me the desired information.

Peggy Brady, of Port Angeles, Washington, once again did her excellent job of reading a rough manuscript and pointing out spelling mistakes and inconsistencies. Tom Beard, of Port Angeles, Washington, caught between 'round the world sailing of *Moonshadow,* read the manuscript and offered excellent suggestions. Truman R. Strobridge, of Alexandria, Virginia, and former historian of the U.S. Coast Guard, also read the manuscript and offered several helpful suggestions. I am, of course, responsible for the content of this book.

Kenneth R. Pott, of the Michigan Maritime Museum, South Haven, Michigan, provided me with access to the museum's collections, plus a great deal of information on the maritime history of the South Haven region. Robert E. Haltiner, chief of resources, Jesse Besser Museum, Alpena, Michigan, provided me with needed information. I spent an interesting morning with Julie J. Pouliot, of the Life-Saving Museum of Virginia, looking at photographs and discussing the USLSS. Wayne Dough, curator, Outer Banks Historical Center, provided me with needed information on Pea Island. The staff of the Center for Great Lakes Research, Bowling Green State University, was extremely helpful. Shirley Whealton, of Tuckerton, New Jersey, provided information on Keeper Jarvis Rider.

Dewey Livingston, of Point Reyes National Seashore, gave me interesting insights into the USLSS in the Point Reyes area. Neal Bullington and Bill Herd, of Sleeping Bear Dunes National Lakeshore, have been of great help in providing information and showing me the outstanding work accomplished on their exhibits dealing with the USLSS. I would recommend a visit to the park for anyone wishing to see one of the best exhibits dealing with the USLSS. Larry G. Points, chief of interpretation at Assateague Island National Seashore, took time out of his busy schedule to assist me and show me the sites of the USLSS within the park. Irene A. Stachura, reference librarian at the San Francisco National Maritime Historical Park, provided me with needed materials.

I extend special thanks to Capt. Gene Davis, U.S. Coast Guard (Ret.), and other members of the staff of the Coast Guard Museum Northwest, Seattle, for their assistance and support.

Capt. T. L. Roberge, U.S. Coast Guard (Ret.), of Port Angeles, Washington, very generously allowed me to examine his family scrapbook and provided me with information about his father, Theodore Roberge, who won the Gold Life Saving Medal.

I would like to thank Paul W. Wilderson, executive editor of the Naval Institute Press, for his help, and other staff members at the press.

I would also like to thank my supervisors at the Institutional Library Services of the Washington State Library, Debra Crumb and Laura Sherbo, for allowing me the necessary time for travel and research.

Glossary of Nautical Terms

Bar. A bank or shoal, usually at the mouth of a river, that makes entry difficult or impossible.

Bark. Usually a three-masted sailing vessel, square-rigged on the fore and main masts and fore-and-aft-rigged on the mizzen (*see* masts).

Beam. The width of a ship or boat.

Bend. Fastening, or tying, one rope to another, usually by passing the rope through a loop and securing it back around its own end.

Boot (*n.*). Recruit.

Centerboard. A movable sliding keel made of wood or metal, pivoting in a fore and aft slot at the forward lower corner. It is raised or lowered by means of a pendant let into the afteredge.

Clinker Built (also clencher built). Boat construction in which the hull planking is fitted overlapping, like shingles on a roof.

Double Banked. Two opposite oars are pulled by rowers seated on the same thwart.

Double Reefed. *See* reef.

Draft. Depth of water that a vessel requires to float freely.

EMIGRANT PACKET. A ship used to regularly carry emigrants, usually from nineteenth-century Europe to the United States.

GUNWALE. The upper edge of a boat's side.

HAWSER. Fiber rope, usually five to twenty-five inches in circumference.

HOOK. Slang for anchor.

HULL. The body of a ship or boat exclusive of masts, yards, sails, rigging, machinery, and equipment.

KEEL. The main center-line structural member, running fore and aft along the bottom of a ship or boat.

LAPSTRAKE. Term applied to boats built on clinker style (*see* clinker built).

LUG FORESAIL. A sail without a boom that is sometimes bent to the foreboom as far as the spar.

MAINSAIL. *See* masts.

MASTS. On three-masted ships, the masts are, after the bow, fore, main, and mizzen.

MIZZEN. *See* masts.

RATLINE. One of the small lines crossing the shrouds (rigging) and forming a ladderlike method for sailors to go aloft on sailing vessels.

REEF. One of the horizontal portions of a sail that may be rolled or folded to reduce the area of canvas exposed to the wind.

RIGGING. All the ropes and other gear used in supporting the masts, yards, booms, gaffs, and sails.

ROCKERED KEEL. A keel with a slight fore and aft curvature; also known as a rocker keel.

SEA DROGUE. A baglike device, usually of canvas, used as a drag to steady a boat in heavy seas.

SCHOONER. A fore-and-aft rigged sailing vessel of two to six masts.

SCOW. A flat-bottomed boat with sloping ends. The bow and stern are square.

SHEER. The longitudinal curvature of the deck at the side between stem and sternpost.

SKIFF. Flat-bottomed, shallow draft, open boat of simple construction, with sharp bow and square stern.

Soundings. To come inshore sufficiently to reach the bottom with a hand lead, which is a device to measure depth.

Sprit Rig. Sail, usually for small boats. A pole set diagonally across a fore and aft sail. The lower end of the sprit rests on a device that encircles the mast.

Sweep Oar. A long, heavy oar used for steering small boats.

Thole Pin. A wooden or steel pin that fits in the hole bored in the gunwale of a rowing boat to keep the oar in place when rowing. The oar may be placed between the two pins.

Thwarts. The benches running across a boat for the crew to sit on.

Transom. The transverse planking that forms the afterend of a small, square-ended boat.

Yawl. Rowboat with stem and stern alike, both ends sharp.

CHAPTER ONE

1880

In 1880, two years after the establishment of the U.S. Life-Saving Service, the crews of the organization faced an unusual year. During this twelve-month stretch of time, two crews received the Gold Life Saving Medal—the highest decoration awarded the civilian lifesavers—all but one member of the station at Point aux Barques, Michigan, drowned in a rescue attempt, and the crew of Point Betsie, Michigan, performed a rescue that is unique in the annals of an organization that performed very daring rescues. One of the dramatic events of the year that culminated in the award of the Gold Life Saving Medal began on 3 February along the gale-swept coast of New Jersey.[1]

The schooner *George Taulane,* bound for New York from Virginia, carrying a deck cargo of cordwood and a crew of seven men, ran into a snowstorm before reaching Sandy Hook. Before attempting the tricky passage into New York's harbor, the captain, a wise seaman, ordered his command to remain offshore in fifteen fathoms of water until the storm passed. Gradually, the wind increased until it reached gale intensity. As the *Taulane* labored heavily, the skipper ordered the mainsail double reefed. At two in the morning the deck cargo shifted and broke free. The hapless crew, in trying to secure the cargo, fought a plunging, heaving ship and dodged the large billets of wood sliding threateningly across the deck. This would seem to have been quite enough problems for the *Taulane,* but this winter night was not yet finished with the ship.[2]

The cry dreaded by all sailors at sea rang out from the forecastle: "Fire!" Flames, fanned by the raging wind, swept quickly through the deck cargo. If the crew had to abandon ship, they faced certain death in the frigid, tossing seas. Somehow the small crew managed to control the fire. With all hands engaged in fighting the conflagration, however, the schooner drifted, slowly and inexorably, toward the beach.

Six hours after the crew of the *George Taulane* began their struggles with fire, wind, and water, in the dim, sleet-filled dawn the beach could be seen no more than one mile away. The skipper, thinking he could save the ship, let go both anchors in an attempt to hold her. But the elements were not yet done with the schooner.

A combination of a strong south current and gale force winds proved too much for the *Taulane*'s hooks, and they began to drag. The ship, now in the trough of the sea, took powerful broadsides from the raging storm. The *Taulane* was rolling heavily, with the seas "making clean breaches over her, staving and rendering, and sweeping everything off her deck"; the sailors were unable to cut the anchor cables. Instead, the men managed "to scramble aloft for their lives." Three of the sailors sought safety in the fore rigging, the remainder of the crew scrambled up the main rigging.

With decks completely awash, the ship gradually began to close the beach, and it appeared the sea was about to claim seven more lives. Then the *Taulane*'s crew spotted the lifesaving crew of Station 11 (Swan Point) following the schooner along the beach. The captain afterward said that "seeing this determined squad gave new life to [my] . . . despairing men."

The crew of the station at Swan Point had earlier spied the *Taulane* approaching the shore. When she dropped her anchors, Keeper James Numan thought the schooner would drag in such a storm and would fetch up closer to Station 12 (Green Island). The keeper then took a gamble: rather than pull the heavy beach apparatus, he ordered his men to grab only heaving lines and to start after the drifting ship. Numan counted on the crew of Green Island to turn out with their cart as soon as they spied the ship. Thus two crews would be on the scene and Numan's surfmen would not be worn out from hauling the heavy beach apparatus. The strategy paid off. The beach patrol of Green Island sighted the *Taulane* and ran back to report to Keeper William P. Chadwick, who immediately ordered out his crew with the beach cart.

The lifesavers faced unusual hazards that cold February night. The tide was four feet higher than normal and the pounding surf surged up to the dune line. The surges cut sluices into the beach, and the sea rushed with uncontrolled energy into these cuts. The seas in the sluices generated enough force to sweep a man off his feet. The beach itself was another hazard. The high water caused the sand to turn to the consistency of quicksand. In addition, the deck cargo of lumber and pieces of the *Taulane* became deadly missiles when hurled ashore by the sea.

The surfmen from Green Island began moving the beach apparatus in the direction of the *Taulane*. The soft condition of the beach made it necessary for the lifesavers to push and pull the cart by hand for about a quarter of a mile. While the surfmen were struggling with the apparatus, Keeper Chadwick gathered a team of horses and met his crew where the beach sand would finally support horses. The team was hitched to the apparatus and the horses pulled steadily for at least a mile. The lifesavers then reached a deep sluiceway and the horses balked. The surfmen grabbed the hauling ropes and pulled the cart through waist-deep water, while keeping a wary eye out for hurling debris and trying to keep their footing. On the other side of the sluiceway, the horses were again hitched up and the trek continued until yet another sluiceway was encountered. Once again, the men went into the water, and from this point on, because the water was "so deep and the sand cut away so fast under the wheels," the surfmen took over the pulling of the cart until they came abreast of the *Taulane*. At this point, the two lifesaving crews finally met. Chadwick's crew was augmented by six civilian volunteers; nineteen men would now attempt the rescue. The hardships the rescuers had endured in just reaching the *Taulane* was merely a prelude to what was in store for them. In the words of the U.S. Life-Saving Service, the nineteen lifesavers now entered into "a singular and memorable struggle."

Four hundred yards offshore the *Taulane* wallowed heavily, its hull almost underwater. Seven crewmen could be seen clinging to the ratlines; one of them was hanging by his arms over a ratline, with one leg through below.

The rescuers placed the Lyle gun atop a small sandhill. It was readied, aimed, and fired. The projectile and shotline flew across the flying jib stay, but the sailors aboard the *Taulane* could not reach it and the men on shore hauled the line and projectile back. In the grip of the surf, the schooner surged further to the south.

The nineteen-man rescue party put everything back onto the beach apparatus cart and hurried after the drifting schooner. The men again set up the Lyle gun. This time the shot fell short. The wet line took on added weight, and the range of the projectile was shortened. The cart was again loaded and the men splashed and staggered with their burden four hundred yards down the beach. The gun was again unloaded from the cart, reloaded with black powder, and fired. This time the shotline parted and the men resumed their exhausting chase.

By now the wheels of the cart had "sanded down," the wheels sunk deep into the wet, soft sand. To prevent the cart from being completely mired, the rescuers had to keep the apparatus in constant motion. At times the cart was partially unloaded and the equipment carried by the rescuers in order to make progress. At other times the men "would . . . fling themselves upon the wheels and hold them with all their strength to prevent the cart from being capsized" in the raging surf. Men were struck by the missilelike debris from the *Taulane*. Chadwick was struck so hard in the right arm by one of these missiles that his right arm was still "lame four months later."

The rescuers chased the *Taulane,* unloaded the cart, and set up the Lyle gun, only to have the ship drift out of range. The crews unloaded and loaded the gun from the cart at "least a dozen times" without getting off a shot. The schooner drifted past Station 12; about a quarter of a mile beyond the station the rescuers saw a chance to fire. Once again, however, the wet shotline parted. By now, the lifesavers and volunteers had been at it for nearly four hours. As the frustrated rescuers retrieved the remnants of the shotline, they saw a sailor from the *Taulane*'s forward rigging fall to his death in the churning seas. Half an hour later, another man dropped from the rigging.

Staggering and floundering onward, spurred by the knowledge that to stop meant certain death for the sailors on the *Taulane,* the lifesavers were dealt another heavy blow. A surge upset the cart and the Lyle gun went into four or five feet of frigid seawater. The men groped in the numbing, thrashing water for the only instrument that could save the men aboard the *Taulane*. The gun was retrieved and wiped dry. One of the keepers—it is not clear which one—hoisted the 165-pound gun onto his shoulder and continued down the beach.

One surfman received orders to run back to Station 12 for dry shotline. As the man hurried to carry out his orders, he heard the fifth shot of the night, but once more the line parted. The keeper again lifted the gun to his shoulder and continued down the beach.

The surfman returned with the dry line just in time; a quarter of a mile further the *Taulane* suddenly struck a north-setting tide, which

Through the raging storm the lifesavers pulled the beach cart, trying to keep pace with the *Taulane*. (From a nineteenth-century illustration in *Harper's Magazine*)

stopped her and swung her bow offshore. "The time had come at last. . . ."

The lifesavers were numb from exhaustion and exposure. But the long hours of monotonous drill paid off as the men automatically set up for another shot. Quickly bending the dry shotline to the projectile, the keeper aimed the Lyle gun and yanked the lanyard. This time the projectile and shotline reached the *Taulane*. The surfmen and volunteers rigged the apparatus. The sailors aboard the *Taulane* grabbed the shotline and pulled the hawser out to the ship. The breeches buoy quickly followed. After the first two sailors were rescued, the schooner grounded, increasing her rolling. The ship rolled so badly that at one time the breeches buoy, with a man in it, swung "fully fifty feet in the air." Even with this carnival-like ride, the last man off the schooner reached safety just thirty minutes after the sailors were able to grab the shotline.

The U.S. Life-Saving Service's official report on the wreck of the *Taulane* notes that the rescuers pursued the ship at least three miles and the entire rescue took "not less than six hours." The nineteen rescuers deservedly received the Gold Life Saving Medal.

A little less than three months later, shortly before sunrise on 23 April, the surfman on lookout at the Point aux Barques Station, Michigan, spotted a distress flag flying from the scow *J. H. Magruder* and sounded the alarm. The station's crew of six surfmen and Keeper Jerome Kiah took up their oars and the boat got underway. Even in protected waters the crew found the lake "moderately heavy."[3] Once the surfboat reached open waters, Kiah later reported, the seas were "heavier . . . than expected, but still not so heavy as we had experienced on other occasions." The *J. H. Magruder* lay approximately a mile and a half away.

After almost an hour at the oars and about a quarter-mile from the ship, Kiah spotted "a tremendous breaker," but did not have time to put the bow of the boat into it. The wave quickly swept over the stern, filling the boat. The boat capsized as the men vainly attempted to bail it out. "We then righted her," said Kiah, "and again were as quickly capsized." The lifesavers again righted the boat and again it capsized. Kiah later related that, "I believe she several times capsized and righted herself after that, but I cannot distinctly remember."

The crew clung desperately to the boat in Lake Huron's frigid water. One surfman dropped away. "I encouraged the men all I could," Kiah recalled, "reminded them that there were others, their wives and children, that they should think of, and to strive for their sakes to keep up, but the cold was too much for them, and one after another each gave out as did the first."

Only Kiah remained:

> I was conscious only at brief intervals. I was not suffering, had no pain, had no sense of feeling in my hands, felt tired, sleepy, and numb. At times I could scarcely see. I remember screeching several times, not to attract attention, but thought it would help the circulation of the blood. I would pound my hands and feet on the boat whenever I was conscious. . . . I remember . . . in [a] dreamy way of when I reached shore.

The service found no fault with Kiah's actions. The superintendent of the Tenth District noted: "Certainly it was the duty of the crew to answer to the signal of distress, and certainly they responded most promptly." The tragedy was "an unfortunate accident." The U.S. Life-Saving Service showed its support of Kiah by awarding him the Gold Life Saving Medal and later promoting him to superintendent of the district.

Some six months later, on 11 October, the schooner *J. H. Hartzell* hove to off Frankfort, Michigan. It would become part of one of the most unusual rescues in the annals of the U.S. Life-Saving Service. Aboard the

Jerome G. Kiah (2d row right), only survivor of the 1880-disaster near Point aux Barques, Michigan, Station; when this photograph was taken he was superintendent of the Tenth U.S. Life-Saving District (Lakes Huron and Superior). (From the Jesse Besser Museum Collection, Alpena, Michigan)

schooner, Capt. William A. Jones commanded a crew of six men and one woman, Lydia Dale, the ship's cook. Captain Jones, being a prudent seaman, opted to lay off until daylight before bringing his ship into harbor. The fresh southeasterly breeze kept the *Hartzell* riding safely offshore. Then, in one of those sudden shifts of weather so common on

Lake Michigan, the wind swung to the southwest and increased to gale force. Hail, snow, and rain lashed the schooner. The howling southwesterly wind and building seas drove the *Hartzell* toward the beach. Captain Jones let go the anchors and ran up the distress flag signals. Three hundred yards from the beach, with her anchors dragging, the *Hartzell* rammed into the bottom.[4]

Captain Jones ordered both anchor cables cut. The ship spun around, her bows pointing toward a range of wooded, sandy bluffs, several hundred feet high. The schooner ground to a halt. The seas began to board the ship, battering everything in their path. The yawl used as a lifeboat was carried away, along with parts of the deck cabin.

The crew took to the rigging to escape the powerful waves. Lydia Dale, recovering from an illness, was carried to the point where the mast and yards join—known as the crosstree. The sailors rigged planks and lashed the cook to the mast. The *Hartzell,* meanwhile, settled by her stern, her bows pointing toward open water. The captain clung to the ratlines ten feet above the lake; the crew and Lydia Dale huddled in the crosstree, forty feet above their skipper. During the official investigation of the wreck, the crew reported hearing the creaking and groaning of the spar trying to break loose from the *Hartzell.*

The son of a fisherman, looking out the window of his cabin, saw the schooner in the surf. The boy ran to his father, who in turn hurried to the village of South Frankfort to give the alarm. Upon receiving the news, a group of at least twenty men rushed across the wooded hills to see if they could assist the shipwrecked sailors.

The first group arrived at eight in the morning, and the number of would-be rescuers swelled as other people arrived either to gawk or to offer assistance. Someone in the crowd suggested a message be fashioned from driftwood to encourage the sailors clinging to the *Hartzell*'s rigging. As this suggestion was being carried out, a messenger mounted a horse and started toward the nearest U.S. Life-Saving Service Station, some ten miles away at Point Betsie. Reining up in front of the station, the messenger rushed inside and informed Keeper Thomas Matthews there was a vessel ashore. Keepers of the U.S. Life-Saving Service were taciturn men and their logbook entries tended to be succinct to the point of being cryptic. The rescue of the *Hartzell,* however, would cause Matthews to write one of the longest log entries in the history of the station.

Normally, the lifesavers would have had a choice of two routes to the wreck site. One was through woods, around the south side of town, across a bridge, and then, finally, to the beach near the stranding. But the second, and shorter, passage near the beach had been closed because of debris tossed ashore by the high waters of the storm. Matthews had to move his equipment over a little-used construction track to reach the main road. A horse was hitched to the station's beach cart and the entire crew, except for the man on patrol, started toward the wreck site.

The track led through thick woods, up and down steep, sandy ravines. The thousand-pound load almost proved too much for the horse. The surfmen were forced to push. The lifesavers reached the main road and immediately encountered a man with a horse and buggy heading to the station. The driver offered to take Matthews ahead to seek a team of horses to pull the cart. Matthews had no more than started off to find a brace of horses, when another man came down the road with a team. The keeper made a decision that proved to be a wise one. He directed that this team go to the Point Betsie Station, be hitched to the surfcar, and then rush to the wreck site. Matthews commandeered a second span of fresh horses, and the lifesavers' equipment covered ten miles in about two hours.

The first sight of the wreck for Keeper Matthews was from a high, sandy bluff a quarter mile from the *Hartzell.* As Matthews was trying to decide how he would transport his equipment over the steep, sandy terrain, a man rode up and stated he knew "a shortcut." The keeper followed.

The suggested route was impassable. It led through a ravine so steep that the team could not pull the loaded cart. Twenty-seven extra men, in addition to the lifesavers and horses, had to pull and tug the apparatus back up to the crest of a hill. A heavily wooded area blocked the way, but the local townspeople began to hack away with axes at the trees. Soon the "hilltop resounded with the blows of implements."

Volunteers and lifesavers then faced yet another obstacle. The beach apparatus had been wrestled through the sands and now stood on the crest of dunes that were towering above the *Hartzell.* Looking downward, Matthews could see the seas washing over the schooner and "the upturned faces" of Captain Jones and his crew. Jones remained clinging to the ratlines, while the remainder of his crew huddled in the crosstree. A crewmember cut some canvas from the shredded sails and wrapped it around Lydia Dale, offering her a little protection from the elements.

From his position on the crest of the dunes, Keeper Matthews spied a ledge some 250 feet below that would make the ideal firing platform. He ordered some of the line from the beach cart unwound and belayed around a tree. Surfmen Barney and Stoker, along with a volunteer, took positions by the shafts of the equipment cart and guided it as it was lowered by the belayed rope.

The cart started downward. The sand kicked up by the men and cart was flung back into the rescuers' faces by the storm. The cart continued downward. Then the belaying line ended. The cart hovered above the ledge. Matthews made another of his "audacious" decisions. Taking the line off the trees, he had a group of volunteers dig their feet into the sand to slow up the cart. The next few seconds can only be described as controlled mayhem. The cart, barely restrained, plunged down the slope. Some of the men were dragged along, still holding gamely onto the line. Miraculously, the cart came to a halt on the ledge and the sweating, begrimed lifesavers now set about readying the Lyle gun for firing.

The surfmen automatically began their routine of setting up the breeches buoy equipment. Keeper Matthews estimated the amount of powder, selected the type of projectile and shotline, determined the elevation, and aimed the gun. The keeper then attached the firing lanyard, yelled "Ready!" and yanked the cord. The shotline landed within easy reach of Captain Jones, but the line lay fouled within the scattered wreckage. Matthews adjusted the Lyle gun and fired a second shot. As the report of the gun echoed off the sand dunes, the shotline sailed over the crosstree where the majority of the crew was huddled.

The sailors aboard the *Hartzell* pulled out the whip. From the shore, the main mast seemed ready to give way and the hull began to break up. Matthews recorded this moment in his log: "I dared not get a hawser out for fear of pulling the mast out of line; if we get them at all, it must be done with the single whip and very soon as the hull is breaking up." (The single whip is the lighter line used to pull the breeches buoy along the hawser.)

The rescue lines, meanwhile, were fouled in the debris of the wreck and it took an hour of intense work to clear everything. At last Matthews had the breeches buoy rigged using only the whip. Just at this moment the lifesaver with the surfcar arrived and it was belayed to the beach in the same manner as the beach cart.

The rescuers on shore were barely able to make out figures on the *Hartzell*. A man crawled into the breeches buoy and began the ride over the storm-tossed lake. It took seventeen minutes to transport the first mate, John Cassidy, to the beach. He stood dazed, not seeming to comprehend that he was, indeed, safe. Cassidy was given brandy while Matthews attempted to get from him an accurate count of the people aboard the

A line was belayed around a tree and the heavy beach cart was lowered down the steep dune. (Drawing by Donald G. McGibbon, Jr.)

ship. During this questioning the keeper learned there was a woman aboard. The news spread quickly through the crowd of onlookers.

It was now approaching three in the afternoon, with little daylight remaining. Darkness and the continuing storm would make the rescue doubly difficult. Matthews confided to his log that he knew drastic measures were needed, so he "took the desperate chance of sending out the lifecar by the single whip."

The lifesaving crew began to pull the lifecar across the lake. The life-

The cart plunged down the dune, dragging surfmen and volunteers behind it. (Drawing by Donald G. McGibbon, Jr.)

car hit the breakers, flipped over, and was tossed about "like a cockle-shell." Finally it was hoisted to the crosstree. Two figures were seen entering the hatch and the signal was given to bring the lifecar back to the beach.

The lifecar arrived in the surfline and Surfman La Core worked at the hatch, which was badly bent by the battering it had taken alongside the wreckage of the *Hartzell*. La Core was repeatedly knocked down by the pounding surf as he tried to free the hatch. At last he succeeded in opening the hatch. The lifesavers and onlookers were surprised to find two sailors emerging without Lydia Dale. The rescued sailors, according to the official report of the wreck, "evasively" informed the keeper that the woman could not make this trip; she was unconscious and would be helped on the next trip.

Again the metal lifecar was sent out, and again the crowd could dimly make out figures moving slowly in the distance. The metal device came back and La Core took another beating from the pounding surf. This time Captain Jones and another man emerged from the car. Now, according to the U.S. Life-Saving Service's report and Matthew's log, "violent murmurs" were heard from the crowd. The keeper later related that he

Knocked about by the waves, Surfman La Core struggled to open the hatch of the lifecar after it returned from the *Hartzell*. (Drawing by Donald G. McGibbon, Jr.)

felt, with darkness fast approaching, there was "little hope of . . . [the lifecar] reaching the mast again," but he ordered another try.

Matthews kept the lifecar at the masthead for a long time, to allow Lydia Dale to be helped into the device. Finally the keeper ordered the return of the car. La Core took another beating from the surf. Lydia Dale was not in the lifecar. Matthews wrote that the crowd was now becoming "surly" and there were cries of: "Where is the woman?" The crowd pressed in on the rescued sailors. Matthews then stepped in and began to interrogate the men. The U.S. Life-Saving Service carefully recorded this questioning:

> "Why didn't you bring back the woman?"
>
> "The woman is dead."
>
> "Be careful now, if you don't know for certain that she is dead, say so; and if you do know, say so."
>
> "The woman is dead, and stiff as a board. She's been dead for some time."

With twilight approaching, Matthews faced a difficult decision: should he send the car out with one of his men in it to see if Lydia Dale was dead? He decided not to. Later the keeper testified that the chance of losing more lives was too great and he reluctantly halted operations. People in the crowd offered the lifesavers rooms for the night, and La Core received medical treatment for injuries sustained from the pummeling received in the heavy surf.

The mast of the *Hartzell* fell during the night. When Matthews viewed the wreck at first light, he saw no trace of either the stick or Lydia Dale's body. The lifesavers gathered up their gear and began trudging back to the station. Lydia Dale's body washed up on the beach seventeen days later.

Was Lydia Dale really dead? Or did the crew of the *Hartzell* ignore the ancient rule of the sea: women and children first? No one will ever know. The sailors of the *Hartzell* stuck to their story that she had died some time before the rescue attempt. The opinions of the local residents, however, can be gleaned from a letter written by First Mate John Cassidy to the *Frankfort Weekly Express* explaining why the crew of the *Hartzell* left the area so quickly. Cassidy felt the citizens of Frankfort "would have tarred and feathered us, if we had not left when we did." Lydia Dale was buried near where she died, and the strange case of her death and the wreck of the *J. H. Hartzell* are largely forgotten.

Who were these crews of lifesavers that fought almost impossible odds to rescue strangers in distress, even giving up their lives to push out into the raging sea? How did these forgotten heroes live? What equipment did they use to carry out their mission? How did the federal government come to have a rescue organization that was devoted to saving lives close to shore? And why did it disappear?

CHAPTER TWO

"An Appropriation of a Very Unusual Kind": The Volunteer Years

Seaborne trade played an important role in the economy of the young United States. In addition to trade goods, a flood of humanity entered America as emigrant packets brought the huddled masses to the shores of the New World. The large number of ships plying the waters of the United States also brought about a somber reality: the death of sailors and passengers due to shipwreck. Many family Bibles register the names of relatives lost along the United States' coastline, but several generations have passed without the dreadful cry "Ship Ashore!"

It is difficult now to imagine ships running onto the beach, resulting in the loss of hundreds of lives. During the early nineteenth century, however, this was not an uncommon occurrence. The federal government's reaction to these losses was the formation of a small organization whose sole purpose was to launch small boats from shore-based stations to rescue those in distress close to the beach. The U.S. Life-Saving Service, which would eventually merge with the U.S. Revenue Cutter Service to form the U.S. Coast Guard, was established in fits and starts.

Dennis R. Means notes the process was the result "of a slow, tedious, reactionary legislative process" and culminated "not on shores swept by storm tides and gales but on the floor of Congress."[1] The story of the formation of the service is also the story of technology at sea and the struggle over whether the federal government or the private sector should control an organization dedicated to helping the public.

Those who go down to the sea in ships have always faced danger. Windjammers faced their greatest danger when they came onto soundings. In the eighteenth and nineteenth centuries large portions of the United States' eastern seaboard were sparsely populated. Furthermore, until near the end of the nineteenth century there were few aids to navigation in this country. For example, in 1852 only 331 lighthouses dotted our coastline.[2] Thus skippers of sailing ships could not depend on a network of lighthouses or buoys to help guide them into a port. Added to the dangers brought about by inadequate aids to navigation, most skippers in the coastal trade, and on the Great Lakes, navigated by coasting. That is, they sailed close to the beach and sought out landmarks to fix their position. A sudden onshore gale could catch a careless captain unawares and drive his craft aground.

The topography of the East Coast also worked against those in the maritime trade. Examine a nineteenth-century nautical chart for the approaches to New York Harbor. A sailing ship makes a long funnel-like approach to the busy port, with the coast of New Jersey on the one hand and the coast of Long Island on the other. Both coasts are noted for sandbars of various depths and directions. Along the New Jersey coast these bars lie at least three hundred to eight hundred yards offshore. Any wooden ship driven onto one of the bars in a storm usually went to pieces within a few hours. Few people can survive a three-hundred-yard swim in forty-degree storm-tossed surf. Even those who made it to the beach stood a good chance of perishing from exposure on the largely uninhabited shore. Once technology provided steam as the main propulsion in ships, avoiding the sandbars was easier, and the force of the wind did not play as critical a role as it did during the Age of Sail. The nature of technology at sea, therefore, played an important role in the establishment of a shore-based rescue service. Once ships were no longer wooden and powered by the wind, the need for a shore-based rescue service for large ships would decrease.[3] Before that time, however, the dangers facing ships entering New York Harbor are well illustrated by the fate of the American bark *Mexico*.

The *Mexico,* after a long and stormy passage from Liverpool, England,

An unidentified wreck. Many nineteenth-century ships sailed close to shore, necessitating short-range rescue techniques. (U.S. Coast Guard)

arrived off the New Jersey coast on New Year's Day 1837, with 112 seasick emigrants aboard. Capt. Charles Winslow signaled for the pilot, as the *Mexico* began to work past Sandy Hook, New Jersey. But this was the Sabbath; there would be no pilot.[4]

The winds of an approaching blizzard began buffeting the *Mexico*. Captain Wilson fought to keep his ship in deep water, but by dusk he knew his ship badly needed assistance. He fired off his distress rockets.

Would-be rescuers on the shore spotted the distress signal, but did not want to risk the now-violent sea. Toward dawn, with the seas at their greatest height, the *Mexico* began her inexorable drift toward shore. At 5:00 A.M., on 2 January 1837, she struck heavily at what is now Long Beach, New York. All hands aboard were lost.

The technology of the eighteenth and nineteenth centuries decreed that specially designed, small oar-powered boats were the best craft to work in the heavy surf close to shore. (This topic is discussed in more detail in chapter 4.) A sailing ship attempting to help stood a very good

The loss of the *Mexico* in 1837 contributed to the formation of the U.S. Life-Saving Service. (Mariner's Museum, Newport News, Virginia)

chance of also running aground, especially if there were strong onshore winds and a heavy surf. The first U.S. shore-based lifeboat station designed to launch small boats for those in distress close to the beach was built in 1807 at Cohasset, Massachusetts, by the Massachusetts Humane Society, a volunteer lifesaving organization. The society established a series of small shedlike structures holding rescue equipment to be used by volunteers in the event of a wreck. The stations, however, were located only near the approaches of a few busy ports; thus large gaps of the coastline remained without lifesaving equipment.[5]

The federal government entered the shore-based lifesaving business in 1848 through the efforts of Congressman William A. Newell, of New Jersey's Second Congressional District. Several years before his election to Congress, Newell, a physician, was on a call in the beach vicinity of Barnegat Inlet, New Jersey. Dr. Newell witnessed the aftermath of the wreck of the bark *Terasto* and the death of thirteen crewmen. The ship stranded on a bar too far away from the beach for the local populace to assist the doomed sailors.

The wreck apparently made a deep impression on Newell, for shortly after he was elected to Congress in 1847, he introduced a resolution calling for the House Committee on Commerce to investigate whether the federal government might assist those in distress along the coasts of his district. At that time the coastal region of the congressman's district went from Sandy Hook in the north (at the approaches to New York Harbor) to Little Egg Harbor Inlet about halfway down New Jersey's coast (about twenty miles above what is now Atlantic City).

Newell's resolution failed to pass. Eight months later, on 3 August 1848, he introduced an amendment to a lighthouse appropriation bill proposed by Congressman Joseph Grinnell of Massachusetts. Congress, eager to adjourn and not wishing to be tied up in a long debate, unanimously passed the amendment on 14 August 1848. The amendment, in part, allotted ten thousand dollars to provide "surf boats, rockets, carronades, and other necessary apparatus for the better protection of life and property from shipwrecks on the coast of New Jersey between Sandy Hook and Little Egg Harbor." This legislation also called for officers of the U.S. Revenue Marine (USRM)—later called the U.S. Revenue Cutter Service (USRCS)—of the Treasury Department's Revenue Marine Bureau to supervise the construction of the stations. The amendment set into action a chain of events that would lead to the formation of the U.S. Life-Saving Service and eventually the U.S. Coast Guard.[6]

The topography and the approaches to New York Harbor, as well as the technology of the times, made the coast of New Jersey a logical choice to begin a federal lifesaving service. In his address to Congress, Newell used a number of statistics to support the need for federal assistance to his district. He stated that from 12 April 1839 to 31 July 1848 a total of 338 shipwrecks occurred on the approaches to New York Harbor. Very close to half, 158, went ashore on New Jersey's coastline. Political and economic factors, however, probably counted more toward establishing the first stations in New Jersey than the number of shipwrecks. The Outer Banks of North Carolina, the infamous Graveyard of the Atlantic, had as many, if not more, wrecks than New Jersey. Why not start the service in North Carolina?

At the time New York City was the fastest growing port in the United States. Anything that interfered with its trade would be politically unwise, and commercial interests and marine insurance companies were willing to support Newell's efforts to establish stations in New Jersey, rather than efforts to build units along the remote beaches of North Carolina. The powerful influence of New York City's politicians and the unique position of New Jersey's Second Congressional District had more to do with where the first federal lifesaving stations were established than how many ships went ashore or how many lives were lost.[7]

On 22 August 1848 Stephen Pleasonton, of the Treasury Department's Fifth Auditor's Office, wrote to Secretary of the Treasury Robert J. Walker that in the "lighthouse law passed on the last day of the late session of Congress, is an appropriation of a very unusual kind, and I now have the honor to bring it to your attention in order that you may take such action on it as may appear to be proper." Pleasonton's communication began the implementation of Congressman Newell's plan for lifesaving stations in New Jersey. Under the supervision of the New York Board of Underwriters and Capt. Douglas Ottinger, USRM, eight small stations were established in New Jersey. In March 1849 Congress appropriated an additional twenty thousand dollars for six more stations on the New Jersey coast from Little Egg Harbor to Cape May. The stations, according to a report dated 21 May 1849, contained galvanized iron surfboats, metal lifecars, rockets, mortars, lights, lines (ropes), powder, heating stoves, firewood, lanterns, and shovels.[8]

The concept of a federal lifesaving service took hold in Congress. In 1850 a station at Watch Hill, Rhode Island, was added, as well as others along the coasts of the Carolinas, Georgia, Florida, and Texas. Four years later $12,500 was authorized for the purchase of metallic surfboats for use on the Great Lakes. There was, however, a flaw in the federal system.

Congress authorized funds to construct the stations, but failed to authorize the necessary money to place someone in charge of the units or to provide for a paid crew. Just as important, no system of inspectors or regulations ensured that the growing network of stations functioned correctly. The federal government would build and equip a station, then turn it over to a community expecting the locals to maintain the station and provide a crew when a ship went ashore. And the government apparently expected the volunteers to perform correctly without the benefit of practice. Over the next twenty-one years, the issue of government involvement versus volunteers would be at the center of the establishment of a professional lifesaving service.[9]

The idea that the federal government would balk at controlling such an obviously humane organization may seem strange to contemporary Americans. The mistrust of federal control, however, was not out of line with early nineteenth-century American thinking. Federal influence over local matters was anathema to most, if not all, Americans of the early 1800s. Washington is usually made the "heavy" by the few writers who have examined the formative years of the U.S. Life-Saving Service. Indeed, the national government did move slowly and reluctantly to take complete control of the lifesaving network. Each step in accepting responsibility for the units was usually the result of a major maritime catastrophe that forced lawmakers to react to public outcries for federal assistance. Most writers infer that if Washington had taken over at the beginning, many lives might have been spared. There is merit in this argument.

On the other hand, other countries, notably England, had excellent volunteer lifesaving services. Furthermore, most of the early U.S. lifesaving stations were established in locations where people made their living from the sea and were knowledgeable in small boat operations. The people in these communities also had a strong tradition of voluntarily helping anyone in distress. With this background, it is perhaps easier to understand the reasoning behind the national government's concept of a volunteer lifesaving system.

In 1854 the symptoms of weakness in the lifesaving network began to appear. A public outcry arose over the loss of more than two hundred lives aboard the emigrant packet *Powhatten* on 16 April 1854. This cry of anguish was prompted, in part, because the ship had grounded near Beach Haven, New Jersey, some six miles from a lifesaving station, and yet there was still a high loss of life. Hannibal Hamlin, chairman of the Senate Committee on Commerce, requested that the secretary of the treasury provide information on the status of the lifesaving stations. Secretary of the Treasury James Guthrie replied that once built, the responsibility for the stations passed from the federal government, but he suggested that the Treasury Department should appoint men to take care of, or keep, the stations and superintendents to supervise the keepers and stations along the New Jersey and Long Island coasts. After another disaster, the loss of 230 lives aboard the *New Era* in November 1854, Guthrie's recommendations were adopted. An act passed on 14 December 1854 authorized keepers of stations to be paid no more than two hundred dollars per year, but no appropriation was made to carry out this act until 1857.[10]

The years 1857 to 1858 saw what at first appeared to be large advances in the lifesaving system. In 1857 Congress authorized $24,185 for salaries, and in 1858 another $26,440 was earmarked for better boats and stations in New Jersey, Long Island, and Galveston, Texas. Stations were repaired and, in general, a revamping of the network took place.[11] Nevertheless, a weakness persisted within the system. As one New Jersey waterman related, the "only person on duty was a keeper . . . and if he discovered a vessel in distress he had to collect a volunteer crew. Along the wilds of Barnegat Beach a keeper would have to tramp miles before he could get a crew together, and perhaps by the time they reached the station, the vessel would be broken up and all hands lost."[12]

The decade following 1858 may rightfully be called the nadir of the lifesaving network. The Civil War interrupted any thoughts of improving the system, and the whole effort languished after the war, although there were some sporadic efforts to bring about changes. In 1866 Congressman Newell once again convinced Congress to authorize money, ten thousand dollars, for new stations. The new units were in the same section of New Jersey where the service had begun eighteen years earlier. Three years later the New Jersey State Legislature attempted to have Congress fund the employment of crews at the stations, but the effort failed. A substitute bill, however, was passed in 1870 that provided for six experienced surfmen to man alternate stations along the New Jersey coast from 15 December to 15 March, with each crewman earning forty dollars per month. In general, however, the system deteriorated. Equipment was stolen, allowed to rust, or used in strange ways. One town, for example, used its lifeboat "alternately as a trough for mixing mortar and a tub for scalding hogs."[13]

The years 1870 to 1871 were pivotal in the establishment of a professional U.S. Life-Saving Service. During the winter of 1870–71 a series of strong storms swept the Great Lakes and the East Coast, resulting in great loss of life. The deaths graphically illustrated the extent of inept personnel, inadequate stations and equipment, and the long distances between stations. The *New York Herald* called for reform to "check the terrible fatalities off our dangerous coast" and to revamp the service so mariners in distress could depend upon help "in the future."[14] Congress responded with a huge two hundred thousand dollars to "employ crews of experienced surfmen at such stations and for such periods as . . . [the secretary of the treasury] might deem necessary and proper . . . for . . . more effectively securing life and property on the coast of New Jersey and Long Island."[15]

In the closing months of 1870, Secretary of the Treasury George S. Boutwell began a search for a reform-minded man to head the department's Revenue Marine Bureau. Dennis R. Means notes that by this time the bureau's revenue cutters had "become little more than pleasure yachts of public men."[16] By February 1871, Boutwell's search had narrowed to a thirty-six-year-old lawyer and former politician from Maine, Sumner Increase Kimball. Kimball was a ten-year veteran of the Treasury Department. He had started in the department as a clerk and, on 1 September 1869, had attained the position of chief clerk in the Second Auditor's Office. His selection by Boutwell to head the bureau marks the beginning of the end of the volunteer era of lifesaving in the United States.[17]

The few general histories of lifesaving in this country have been less than generous toward the efforts put forth during the period from 1848 to 1871. Keepers are usually pictured as political appointees, more adept at currying favor with the in party than at handling an oar. And the weakness of depending on volunteers, with no supervision or drills, was indeed a flawed practice. Definite problems with the volunteer organization existed, but some good did come out of the period, primarily the federal government's entry into the shore-based rescue business. Without the financial resources available to the government, it is doubtful that our coastline would have been as well protected. Private societies did the best within the limits of their resources, but the vast coastline of the United States could not have been adequately financed by donations. Political decision-makers realized that the federal government would have to take a part in lifesaving and maritime safety. This led in 1869 to the creation within the Treasury Department of the Division of Revenue Marine, which included revenue cutters, the lifesaving stations, steamboat inspectors, and marine hospitals.[18]

Another important feature of the volunteer era that would help in the federal period was the development of a group of trained surfmen who could handle the boats and equipment needed to perform rescues of shipwrecked sailors. These men would help provide the cadre needed for the new service.[19]

The appointment of Sumner Increase Kimball to head the Treasury Department's Revenue Marine Bureau in 1871 marks the end of the federal government's experiment in a volunteer lifesaving service. Kimball would take a badly managed organization and inject his own managerial skills, forming in time one of the more respected and noble undertakings of any government. The volunteer era has usually been depicted as being, at best, misguided and, at worst, actually dangerous to those shipwrecked on the coasts of the United States. The volunteer organization's shortcomings proved to Kimball that a truly professional lifesaving service required a strong centralized organization that stretched over local and state boundaries.

CHAPTER THREE

The Kimball Years: 1871–1914

The appointment of Sumner Increase Kimball to head the Treasury Department's Revenue Marine Bureau has been called the "single most important event" in the history of the U.S. Life-Saving Service, for the lifesaving stations were placed in Kimball's bureau.[1] Under Kimball's leadership the basic foundations of the service were laid between the years 1871 and 1878. The organization that he established during this time required only a few periodic adjustments over the entire span of the service. Many of the operational procedures established in this seven-year period would last well into the era of the U.S. Coast Guard and, indeed, some are still relevant. The major issues that Kimball faced during his tenure as the general superintendent of the U.S. Life-Saving Service were personnel and the efficient operation and expansion of the service.

When Kimball was offered the opportunity to head the Revenue Marine Bureau, he wrote Secretary of the Treasury George S. Boutwell that he would accept the responsibility "upon one condition": the secretary should stand by his new appointee's decisions on reforms, as "Congressmen will come to you in long processions and will attempt to convince you that the service is being ruined." Kimball went on to say that Boutwell would require "an uncommon display of backbone," but if the secretary would back him, Kimball promised he would put the bureau "where you want it and where it ought to be." Boutwell responded that "no matter what the pressure may be I shall not interfere."[2]

Two months after taking up his new duties, Kimball ordered Capt. John Faunce, USRM, to inspect every lifesaving station and report on its condition. The new head of the Revenue Marine Bureau (later called the Revenue Marine Division) accompanied Captain Faunce on some of the visits. Faunce's orders were to describe the equipment and the type of men serving at the units. The captain's 9 August 1871 report painted a dismal picture. Stations "were too remote from each other, and . . . [the] houses were much dilapidated, many being . . . worthless. . . . With but few exceptions, . . . they were in a filthy condition" and, in general, "gave every evidence of neglect and misuse." The equipment in some cases had been stolen; if in place it showed lack of care and maintenance. Many keepers were too old for the strenuous work of rescue; others lived too far from the station; others were simply incompetent, with politics having "more influence in their appointment" than the ability to handle a boat. Kimball, armed with Faunce's report and his own administrative abilities, plus a whopping two-hundred-thousand-dollar appropriation from Congress, set out to revamp the network.[3]

Two of Kimball's first priorities were to convince decision-makers that the nation needed a federally controlled, professional lifesaving service and that he was capable of establishing just such an organization. Kimball gathered statistics, then used these data, along with annual reports, to drive home his points. The method in which Kimball used the statistics shows the hand of a man who had spent many years in a bureaucracy. This is also illustrated in his selection of an assistant.

William D. O'Connor became the assistant to the general superintendent of the service in 1878. O'Connor, a Bostonian born in 1832, was a journalist from 1853 to 1859; he gained a reputation both in his field and as a literary writer. He lost his position on the Philadelphia *Saturday Evening Post* for writing favorably about the abolitionist John Brown. He made his way to Washington, D.C., in 1861 and held a series of posts within the Treasury Department, including librarian of the department from 1874 to 1875 and a clerk in Kimball's Revenue Marine Division from 1875 to 1878. Among his circle of literary friends was the poet Walt Whitman. One of O'Connor's most important duties in the U.S. Life-

Capt. John Faunce, USRM; his 1871 report identified weaknesses of the lifesaving system. (Mariner's Museum, Newport News, Virginia)

Saving Service was the preparation of the annual report.[4] The organization that Kimball set in motion funneled the reports and investigations of keepers and inspectors into Washington, D.C., where O'Connor, using his talents as a writer, had the raw material that any writer would love to possess: excitement, adventure, death, heroic rescues—all of it well documented. The annual reports that O'Connor authored, especially the sections that dealt with shipwrecks involving death, are arguably the most exciting reading ever produced by the U.S. government. The annual reports became so popular that additional copies had to be produced.[5] Kimball had on hand an articulate source to promote the service.

Using Captain Faunce's report as his guide, Kimball began to point out how many of the keepers of the volunteer era were inept, many holding their positions through political patronage rather than by virtue of being expert boatmen. The 1876 annual report gives a history of lifesaving in this country and is the source for most of what we know about the volunteer era. O'Connor also authored an entry in *Appleman's Cyclopedia* for 1878, which in large part repeats the annual report and stresses the failure of the volunteer era. Both publications imply that under Kimball there was a clean sweep of the inept keepers. Kimball had to convince Congress that the volunteer era was a failure and what was needed was a strong, paid federal organization.

Robert F. Bennett suggests that Kimball, while not exactly lying, appears "through emphasis and omissions in his published documents, [to] guide the pens of future historians toward a negative evaluation of [the] early organization."[6] This would also apply to guiding the minds of Congress. In 1872 Kimball wrote that during the volunteer era he had "been able to learn with certainty of the rescuing of 4,163 lives and the saving of $716,000.00 worth of property through the instrumentality of this service. There is no reason to believe that these figures would be greatly increased if accurate figures could be obtained." Ten years later the annual report noted that it "has been established in previous reports that during the twenty years preceding the organization of the Service, five hundred and twelve persons are known to have been lost on the Coast of New Jersey and Long Island alone, although if full statistics could be had, the number would be known to be very much greater."[7] The change in wording between the two reports, covering the same period in the volunteer years, might well influence a congressman, particularly considering that by 1882 O'Connor's style would have made the reports more popular.

Bennett also questions Kimball's claims about ridding the service of political appointees. Using personnel records, Bennett writes that "only 6 of the 28 positions on the New Jersey coast changed, and one of those six moved to a new unit."[8] Moreover, in the early 1880s a superintendent advised the keeper of the station at Amagansett, Long Island, to "see that one-half of your crew are Republicans and one-half Democrats as per arrangement made last August by the General Superintendent of the Long Island service."[9] All of this suggests that "Kimball's 'official' claims occasionally proved to be mere rhetoric."[10] By the late 1880s the service was well established, and in 1896 civil service rules took effect and the issue of political appointees became a less heated point.

Favoritism undoubtedly did take place in appointments, and Kimball was right to try to rid the service of these appointees. He no doubt felt that if the U.S. Life-Saving Service was to become a professional organization it would have to rise above petty politics. There is also no doubt that the hiring of O'Connor as the assistant to the general superintendent was a brilliant move on Kimball's part. O'Connor's writing abilities went a long way toward helping to sell the new organization to Congress and the nation. Kimball would certainly use statistics in any manner possible to gain an advantage for his service.

Another important step in improving the operations of the service was to have units located no more than five miles apart. Surfmen would then be able to walk patrols between the stations, thus increasing the chances of detecting ships wrecked on the isolated shoreline. To accomplish this goal new stations were built along the New Jersey and Long Island coasts and older ones repaired. In an age of slow communications Kimball sought ways to improve the speed with which stations were notified of ships in distress. In 1873 an agreement was reached with the U.S. Army Storm Signal Service to establish telegraph lines between the units along the New Jersey coast. Signal Corps enlisted men were allotted space in the stations to perform their work of transmitting weather data. In 1884 Kimball ordered the installation of telephones at nineteen stations along the New Jersey coast and slowly expanded this service to other regions.[11]

In 1873 another one hundred thousand dollars was appropriated for the network, with the stipulation that the secretary of the treasury report where he intended to site newer stations and how much was to be spent expanding the network. This was not an easy directive to carry out, for the locations of wrecks were not accurately recorded. In another excellent organizational move, Kimball went before Congress to seek legislation to allow him to comply with the directive. On 20 June 1874 Congress passed the Life-Saving Stations Act, which included an important stipulation: masters of U.S. vessels were required to report to the collectors of customs all groundings, founderings, capsizings, strandings, fires, and explosions. The ensuing compilation of disasters to U.S. ships provided the justification for the expansion of the stations and helped determine the location of future units. The legislation remains the basis for obtaining reports of marine accidents occurring on all U.S. commercial craft. The act also granted to the secretary of the treasury the right to bestow gold and silver lifesaving medals for specific acts of heroism.[12]

After setting into motion the changes in the lifesaving network, Kimball published *Regulations for the Government of the Life-Saving Service of the United States*. Every aspect of the organization and operational procedures were contained within the forty-five-page book. The regulations were so basic, and so all-encompassing, that only three revisions were made to them during the history of the U.S. Life-Saving Service. The regulations were very basic because the less complicated a procedure was the less chance for confusion or failure. In addition most rescue operations depended on brute strength rather than sophisticated technology; rescue techniques did not require a great deal of complicated instructions. All the boats were oar-powered, and the surfboat and its carriage could be pulled along the beach by the lifesavers. Because the operational procedures were simple, they did not become quickly outdated. Some are still applicable today. For example, the regulations clearly stated that lifesaving crews must practice every week with their equipment. Even today, to be truly proficient in rescue operations, crews must practice constantly.

During 1874 the lifesaving network expanded to the coast of Maine and to ten locations south of Cape Henry, Virginia, including the Outer Banks of North Carolina. The next year more stations were added, this time on the Delaware-Maryland-Virginia peninsula, the Great Lakes, and the coast of Florida. Eventually, the Gulf of Mexico and portions of the West Coast would be included.[13]

Congress began to respond to the efforts to reorganize the lifesaving network, passing important legislation and appropriations. However, not everything went smoothly during the important first seven years. In 1878 a strong effort was made to place the service under the jurisdiction of the U.S. Navy. The wrecks of the *Huron* and *Metropolis* along North Carolina's Outer Banks in 1877 and 1878, with the loss of at least 183 lives, graphically illustrated the remaining deficiencies in personnel and stations. But Kimball's administrative accomplishments overrode these problems. Congress supported the efficient new organization and the effort to transfer the service to the Navy was beaten back. And the problems highlighted by the two terrible shipwrecks had already been pointed out by Kimball in his annual report to Congress. Not surprisingly, on 18 June 1878, when President Rutherford B. Hayes signed the bill creating the U.S. Life-Saving Service as a separate agency within the Treasury Department, Kimball was nominated to be the general superintendent of the service. The Senate rapidly confirmed him.[14]

In the organic act that created the service Kimball was directed "to cause to be properly investigated all plans, devices, and inventions for the improvement of life-saving apparatus for use at the stations, which may appear to be meritorious and available." On 3 January 1882 the secretary of the treasury appointed a Board on Life Saving Appliances that was made up of seven members and included an inspector and assistant inspector of lifesaving stations from the USRM, an officer from the U.S. Army Ordnance Department, two district superintendents of the U.S. Life-Saving Service, and a station keeper.[15]

At times Kimball must have wondered why lawmakers saddled him with this provision. For every "meritorious" invention that crossed his desk, a dozen outrageous contraptions were sent to the board. Take, for example, Aikin's Flying Cannon. Many attempts were made to design a method of passing a line to a distressed ship from the shore, and most proposals, quite naturally, called for propelling the line over the water. Rockets, balloons, and kites were suggested or used. Eventually, a system was developed that shot a projectile with a line attached. Not so Aikin's Flying Cannon. In this instance the entire *cannon* went sailing over the water to the ship. Maj. David Lyle, the ordnance officer assigned to the board, dutifully carried out the testing of this amazing device.

More than a hundred years later one can read Lyle's account and almost see the major trying to decide whether to laugh or throw up his hands in exasperation. In his report he noted that the cannon, in fact, did work as advertised: "The 'flying-cannon' of Mr. Aikin seems to be a new departure in the way of line-carrying projectiles." Lyle went on to note that to the "indefatigable Frenchman, Delvigne, belongs the credit of originating the idea of firing the ramrod out of the gun and utilizing it for carrying a line; but to Mr. Aikin, that of shooting *the gun off the ramrod* for the same purpose." It was a unique idea. As Lyle pointed out, shooting projectiles that might be lost was a more cost-effective method of passing a line to a ship than losing an entire cannon.[16]

Although the service depended largely on human power, Kimball did try to improve the technology, such as by installing telephones. To help speed up the movement of equipment, in 1880 the general superintendent approved the use of horses at stations. In 1899 the U.S. Life-Saving Service began to experiment with gasoline-powered lifeboats.[17]

The service operated under a dual chain of command that reported to Kimball, who reported to the secretary of the treasury. One branch of the chain was civilian; the other was staffed by USRM personnel, headed by a captain, who was stationed in New York City and held the title of inspector of the U.S. Life-Saving Service. The 1873 regulations directed that the inspector and the district superintendent visit each station at least once a year for a thorough examination of the crew. As the service grew, an assistant inspector, usually a lieutenant in the USRM, was appointed to each district. In addition to inspecting station crews, the assistant inspector's duties included investigating wrecks. According to Robert Bennett the assistant inspectors "were the principal innovators in the Life-Saving Service."[18] Most crewmen, he argues, were local residents and wished to preserve the status quo. The inspectors, being subject to transfer, had no ties to the region and were willing to enforce the regulations without worrying about pressure from important local families. Bennett, however, points out that sometimes the assistant inspectors were misguided. One inspector required a crew to man a heavy surfboat in an offshore rescue instead of the traditional lighter model. The crew was so "totally exhausted" that upon their return to the "surfline," they could not prevent the boat from broaching to and "three surfmen died."[19] Nevertheless, without the formal inspections of the assistant inspectors the service might well have remained as it was before 1871.

The civilian side of the chain of command was headed by district superintendents appointed by the secretary of the treasury with Kimball's recommendation. The superintendent was examined by a board made up of two people, one of whom was the inspector of life-saving stations. Superintendents had to be "not less than twenty-five nor more than fifty-five years of age," be able to read and write and "have some knowledge of the elementary principles of bookkeeping." They had to be very familiar with their districts and the use of rescue equipment. In general, district superintendents took care of administrative duties. Superintendents were required to visit all of their stations at least five times a year to check on readiness, cleanliness, and record keeping. They were also responsible for paying the crews and recommending to Kimball appointments to the position of keeper, the official in charge of a station.[20]

Keepers were nominated by the district superintendent, approved by Kimball, and appointed by the secretary of the treasury. The 1873 regulations stated that a keeper would be appointed after being examined by a board composed of three people, one of whom had to be the district superintendent and another a physician. The man selected for this position had to be not less than twenty-one nor more than fifty-five years of age, and able to read and write. He also had to have a "knowledge of notation, numeration, and the four elementary rules of arithmetic." The keeper also had to be an expert in the "management of the surf-boats and of the use of the various apparatus used in the service." The keeper was responsible for all aspects of running the station, including selecting and managing the crew. He was also required to keep a journal, or log, of the station's activities and to file wreck reports. The keeper had as much control over the station as the captain of a ship. In the 1880s qualifications

Charles Morton, who began his thirty-one years of service as a surfman and worked his way up to superintendent of the Eleventh District (Lake Michigan), had served in the U.S. Army at the Battle of the Little Big Horn. (Michigan Maritime Museum, South Haven, Michigan)

to become a keeper were modified somewhat; the most important change was a mandatory annual physical examination. Failure to pass meant forced resignation. This regulation would have far-reaching effects on the service.[21]

The crewmen of the service were known as surfmen, after the East Coast fishermen who launched their boats into the surf from the open beach. The 1873 regulations spelled out no specific requirements for the position, except that the keeper would select "able-bodied and experienced Surfmen residing nearest to the station at which they are to be employed." This rather broad regulation remained in effect until civil service rules were applied in 1896; then keepers chose from a list of best-qualified candidates.

Surfmen were not employed the entire year, except on the West Coast. Wrecks on the West Coast were most likely to occur at the entrance to harbors and at any time of the year; on the East Coast wrecks were more likely to happen during the winter. The surfmen signed "articles of agreement" to serve for what was known as the "active season," when wrecks were most likely to occur. The season at first varied from location to location on the East Coast. In 1876 the season in Maine was from 1 November to 1 April; on the coast of New Jersey from 1 November to 1 April; and along North Carolina's coast it stretched from 1 December to 1 April. By 18 June 1878 the season along all of the East Coast was from 1 September to 1 May. On the Great Lakes the season was usually from about April until November or December when the lakes froze.[22]

The size of the crew depended on the number of oars for the largest boat assigned to the station, usually six. In 1885 a seventh man—known as the winter man—was added to the crews during the busiest period of the active season.[23] This provided extra help during the launching and recovery of boats and ensured that the station would be manned while the crew was engaged in a rescue. At stations where the lifeboat was assigned, mainly on the Great Lakes, the crew size was usually eight. Once the articles of agreement were signed the surfman was assigned a number that signified his rank and experience in the crew; all duties at the station were listed by number. Number one was the senior surfman and second in charge; number six or eight was the least experienced. When the service acquired uniforms in 1889, the rank number was worn on the left sleeve. At the end of the active season the surfman would be discharged; if he had performed his duties correctly he would be hired again the next season.[24]

The keeper remained at the station the entire year and was expected to provide assistance to ships or people in distress, even if he did not have a crew. The service's reports are filled with rescues performed by keepers during the inactive season. One example of the tenacious efforts exerted during an inactive season occurred along the coast of North Carolina.

A rapidly moving hurricane struck heavily at Charleston, South Carolina, during the last days of August 1893. The storm arrived so suddenly that many vessels were caught by surprise. Eight ships, with a total of fifty-five sailors and one passenger, disappeared in the storm. For Keeper Dunbar Davis at the Oak Island Station near Cape Fear, the hurricane would mean a test of his endurance.[25]

At one o'clock in the morning of 28 August 1893 the three-masted schooner *Three Sisters,* of Philadelphia, was near Frying Pan Shoals Lightship when the hurricane's winds struck her. Within an hour her canvas was in ribbons and the mizzenmast was carried away. The master and mate were lost overboard, leaving the cook in charge of the remaining five crewmen.

The *Three Sisters* continued to wallow and drift in the heavy seas. At two in the afternoon the hapless schooner was spotted by Keeper J. L. Watts of the Cape Fear Station and also by Keeper Davis. The seas were running so high that both keepers knew it would be impossible to reach the ship. Watts signaled the schooner to drop anchor and await assistance.

Now the problem for the keepers was how to provide the promised help. Davis and Watts met and talked over a plan of action. Davis would return to the Oak Island Station and prepare his surfboat while Watts tried to find volunteers. By 8:30 P.M. the two keepers and nine volunteers were in the Oak Island Station's surfboat.

In a three-hour battle against strong winds and tides the crew rowed across the mouth of the Cape Fear River and then hugged the coastline until they were opposite the *Three Sisters*. The schooner was riding easily and the two keepers decided to wait for dawn before broaching the high surf. At first light the rescue crew pulled to the anchored ship and it was a "comparatively simple matter" to get the five stranded sailors and transport them to safety at the Cape Fear Station. The *Three Sisters* would be towed in when the storm abated.

The rescue successfully completed, the volunteers left and Watts began to look after the shaken sailors. Then Davis noticed a distress signal flying from the pole at his station. The Oak Island keeper rounded up another group of volunteers, this time finding eight, five of them from the original group. Reaching the Oak Island Station, Davis learned that his wife had run up the distress signal. She had received word that the German brig *Wustrow* had run aground approximately nine miles west of the station. Shortly after Davis learned of this stranding, word reached the Oak Island Station that fishermen had rescued the sailors of the *Wustrow*. To be safe, Davis decided to climb the lookout tower and scan the area before dismissing the volunteers. What he saw from the tower must have made the fifty-year-old keeper pause. There to the west, near where the *Wustrow* had run aground, was another three-masted schooner anchored just beyond the breakers.

Davis and his volunteer crew set out in the surfboat. This time the force of the wind and surf held them in an almost "stationary position" no matter how hard they pulled at their oars. The boat was forced to run for shelter.

A pilot boat and tug had come to the area after learning about the strandings. Davis asked the captains of both vessels to tow his boat across the heavy breakers and into open water. Both skippers refused. This left only one course of action: the rescue crew would have to return to the station and transport the heavy line-throwing equipment along the beach. By this time, the crew had gained another volunteer, one of the regular active-season men. The beach was cut through in many places, and the rescuers made slow time. Davis then saw that the ship was not aground and he unloaded the cart, hoping to be of some help to the crew. After struggling on for another two miles, the keeper came upon a man with a mule and cart. The man informed Davis that the crew of the *Wustrow* had found shelter in a farmhouse and a party of fishermen was taking everything that washed ashore.

Davis hired the man with the cart to take him ahead of the toiling volunteers so he could assess the situation at the *Wustrow* site. Arriving there, he found that the ship he had spied from the lookout tower had tried to get underway but had grounded. Davis sent the man and his cart back to the volunteer crew to help speed up the transport of the equipment. "Even with the mule's help we could make but little headway, for the sand was boggy and every half mile or so we would come to deep gullies," Davis later reported. Keeper Davis and his volunteer crew came upon extra help in the form of another man with a yoke of oxen. As they were hitching the beasts to the equipment cart, Keeper Watts arrived with five additional volunteers. The reinforced party finally arrived at the shipwreck site at two in the morning. In the darkness of predawn the rescuers set up the line-throwing equipment, fired the gun, and started landing the stranded sailors.

By the afternoon of 30 August 1893 Keeper Davis had gone to the assistance of three ships and helped save twenty-one sailors. "By this time I was getting pretty fagged," Davis later admitted. "I had gone without food for two days and without water for 12 hours, and had been wet all the time." When he finally arrived at his station, he found all the beds filled with castaways and all the food gone. Fortunately, the keeper of a nearby lighthouse and his wife brought over additional food. Thus ended two long days of the inactive season of Keeper Dunbar Davis of the Oak Island Station.

The 1871 report Captain Faunce submitted to Kimball on the condition of the lifesaving network noted that the distance between stations was too great. One of the first moves in revamping the organization was to bring the stations along the New Jersey and Long Island coastlines closer together by constructing new units or renovating older stations. At about the same time, Kimball moved to classify the stations of the service and to bring architectural order to the construction of new units. Along New Jersey's shoreline a dozen new twelve-by-eighteen-foot two-story houses were ordered, along with modifications of the existing twenty-eight units. On Long Island six new stations were completely demolished, then rebuilt at their original locations. The new Long Island and New Jersey stations were forty-two feet long by eighteen feet wide, with shingled roofs and sides. They were known as red houses because of their color scheme.[26]

As the lifesaving network grew, more attention was given to architecture. Eventually, the service employed professional architects and the stations reflected the styles of the men who designed them. The stations were "plain, yet picturesque" and fit well into the seaside communities where they were built, which was a good community relations plan. Many stations came to resemble beach-front cottages, and communities took pride in their lifesaving stations. The design for the station at Bay Head, New Jersey, featured a clock tower; the clock was donated by the community.[27]

With the official establishment of the U.S. Life-Saving Service in 1878 the service's stations were divided into three classes. The first class consisted of complete lifesaving stations and "were distinguished from those of all other classes by the presence of regularly employed crews of surfmen, and by being built as domiciles, and for the temporary accommodation of shipwrecked persons." The lifesaving stations were typically two-story affairs, built of tongue-and-groove pine, with gable roofs, covered with cypress or cedar shingles, and strong shutters on the

Townsend Inlet, New Jersey; one of the early stations along the East Coast. (U.S. Coast Guard)

windows. Roughly in the style of a chalet, early stations had an open platform on the roof, which evolved into an enclosed lookout tower. The exterior walls were painted drab, with darker color for the door and window trimmings, and the roofs were dark red. The doors of the boathouses faced the sea and had a small ramp that led to the beach. A sign that read U.S. Life-Saving Station hung over the boathouse door. Lifesaving stations were eighteen to twenty feet wide and forty to forty-five feet long. Two-thirds of the ground floor space was given over to the boatroom, with the remaining space used as a living area for the crew. The second floor was divided into rooms for the keeper and crew, and for storage.[28]

The next class, lifeboat stations, were usually located on the Great Lakes and the Pacific Coast. Most of the shipwrecks in these regions occurred at the entrance to harbors and the service placed the lifeboat stations within the harbors, close to where wrecks were most likely to occur. These units were usually one-and-a-half stories high, twenty-two

Open house held in 1883 at Deal, New Jersey. Originally just shedlike constructions, stations became more elaborate over the years, and a special relationship developed between the service and nearby communities. (U.S. Coast Guard)

feet wide and forty-two feet long, with a single room on the first floor for the lifeboat and other rescue gear, and a small loft. The buildings were constructed of the same material and painted with the same colors as lifesaving stations. The heavy lifeboats could be launched either through a trap door, if the station was built on pilings, or down a ramp. The sign over the boathouse door read U.S. Life-Boat Station. Originally, lifesaving stations, because of their remoteness, were the only units that kept crews at the station. Lifeboat stations relied on the keepers' finding volunteer crews in the neighborhood. As time passed, however, even lifeboat stations began to keep paid crews on site.

Stations located in Georgia, South Carolina, and portions of Florida made up the third class, known as houses of refuge. In this region ships "come up almost high and dry, rendering comparatively easy the escape of their crews, whose chief liability, . . . is to perish from hunger and

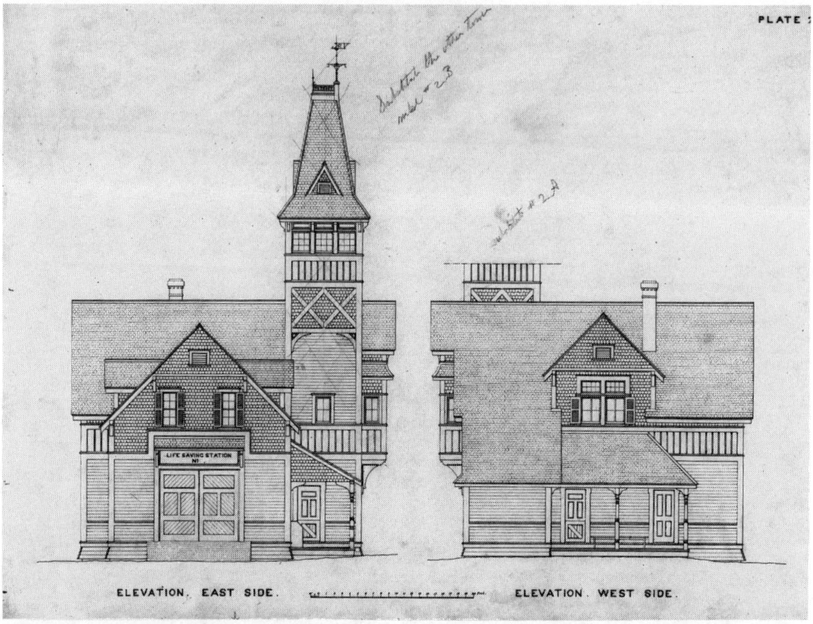

Drawings for the station at Bay Head, New Jersey. (Center for Cartographic and Architectural Archives, National Archives)

thirst." Houses of refuge were crewed by a keeper and his family, who would patrol the beaches after a storm. The houses could hold up to twenty-five survivors, with provisions for ten days. The building was fifteen-by-thirty-seven feet with three rooms on the first floor and a loft. According to one account the units were "of a style common in the South, with broad gabled roofs, an ample veranda 8 feet wide on three sides of the structure, and large chimneys in the rear, built outside the wall." The houses were built of pine, raised about six feet from the ground on light wooden posts; the roofs were shingled with cypress. Instead of glass, the windows were "fitted with wiregauze mosquito netting."

New station locations were determined either by petition to the U.S. Life-Saving Service by communities or by the statistics gathered by the act of 1874, which mandated that maritime disasters be reported, thus providing information about where shipwrecks were most likely to occur. The amount of land used by the service was relatively small. In many cases the land was donated to the service. Free land, however, was not without its problems. Charles Webb Howard, for example, donated a

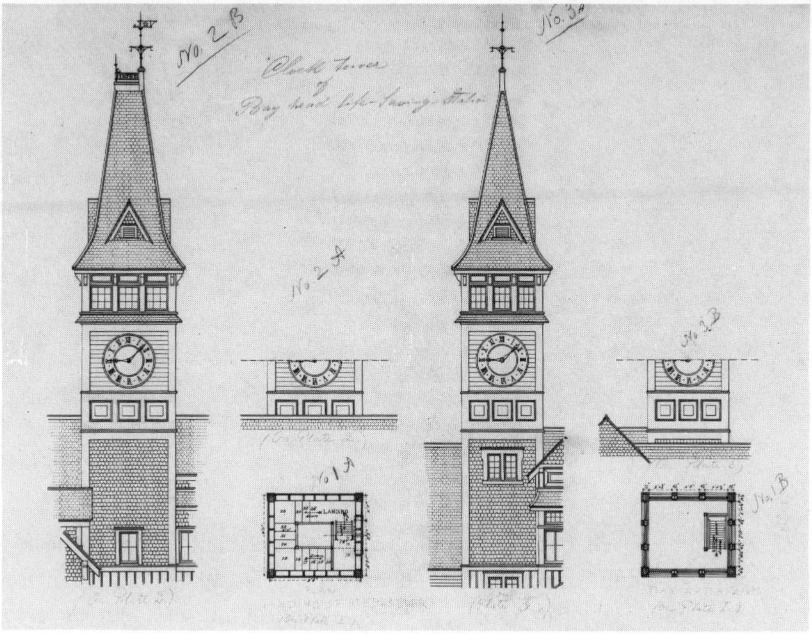

The community donated the clock for the Bay Head station's tower. (Center for Cartographic and Architectural Archives, National Archives)

three-and-a-half-acre site for the station at Point Reyes, California. Assistant Inspector C. H. McClellan was soon writing to headquarters that Howard was causing "vexatious delays" by constantly changing his mind. McClellan wrote that "several times I considered the business satisfactorily settled, when after thinking the matter over night Mr. How-

The station at Cape Lookout, North Carolina, with its enclosed lookout tower atop the roof is typical of units along the isolated eastern seaboard. (U.S. Coast Guard)

Station at San Francisco's Golden Gate Park. (U.S. Coast Guard)

ard whould [*sic*] change his mind and the work would have to be repeated." Normally, the deed would have been sent to Washington for approval, but McClellan approved the transaction himself. In a letter to Kimball, he wrote: "[Howard] has played fast and loose with me so long (since 23d of Dec. [1887]) that I dare not allow the time necessary to

Station at Deer Park, Michigan; many stations had dogs as mascots. (Center for Cartographic and Architectural Archives, National Archives)

The well-tended grounds of the unit at Frankfort, Michigan. (U.S. Coast Guard)

send the deed on to Washington." Kimball backed his assistant superintendent.[29]

Once the site had been accepted, the service then put out bids to local contractors, who followed the very detailed *Instructions for the Construction of a Life-Saving Station*. These instructions ensured that the stations would be built in the most cost-effective method. Although the units were generally standardized versions, closely resembling one another, some stations were unusual because of location, type of station, or other features.

The service operated one station outside the contiguous United States, at Nome, Alaska. Because of the shallow waters of the Bering Sea, deep draft seagoing ships cannot reach the harbor of Nome. Vessels must lie one or two miles offshore in an open roadstead, with cargo and passengers lightered by barge or small boat. The Bering Sea is noted for sudden changes in weather, and any increase in wind velocity can quickly whip the shallow waters to dangerous heights for small boats. In 1899 nine people were drowned during the transfer from ships to the beach; in 1900, fourteen lives were lost.[30]

In 1899 the U.S. Revenue Cutter Service detailed a boat crew from the USRCS cutter *Bear,* which cruised the Bering Sea, to provide lifesaving assistance to Nome. This summer routine continued for the next seven years. Congress authorized the establishment of a station at Nome as early as 1900 and appropriated two thousand dollars for equipment. No

Details on the station building at Chicago include lifebuoy with crossed boat hooks, the service's logo. (U.S. Coast Guard)

money, however, was appropriated to pay for a crew. In 1903 the boundary of the Thirteenth Lifesaving District was extended to include Nome, and in 1905 Congress appropriated funds for the station, which officially opened on 25 August 1905. The station was open only during the summer as Nome lies well north of the winter sea ice limits. The boathouse was destroyed in a fire in 1903, and a new structure was erected in 1914. Changes in shipping, the end of the gold rush, and other factors prompted the officer in charge of the station in 1934 to recommend that the unit be placed in a reduced commission status. The final fate of the station was settled on 17 September 1934 when a fire totally destroyed twelve city blocks of downtown Nome, including what was then the U.S. Coast Guard Station. The station was not rebuilt. Thomas A. Ross, whose tenure extended from 1905 to 1934, was the sole keeper of the Nome unit. The U.S. Coast Guard did acquire new facilities in Nome during World War II, but these were abandoned in 1949.

Many of the service's units were in isolated areas. The lookout tower at Sleeping Bear Point, Michigan, was detached from the main building. (U.S. Coast Guard)

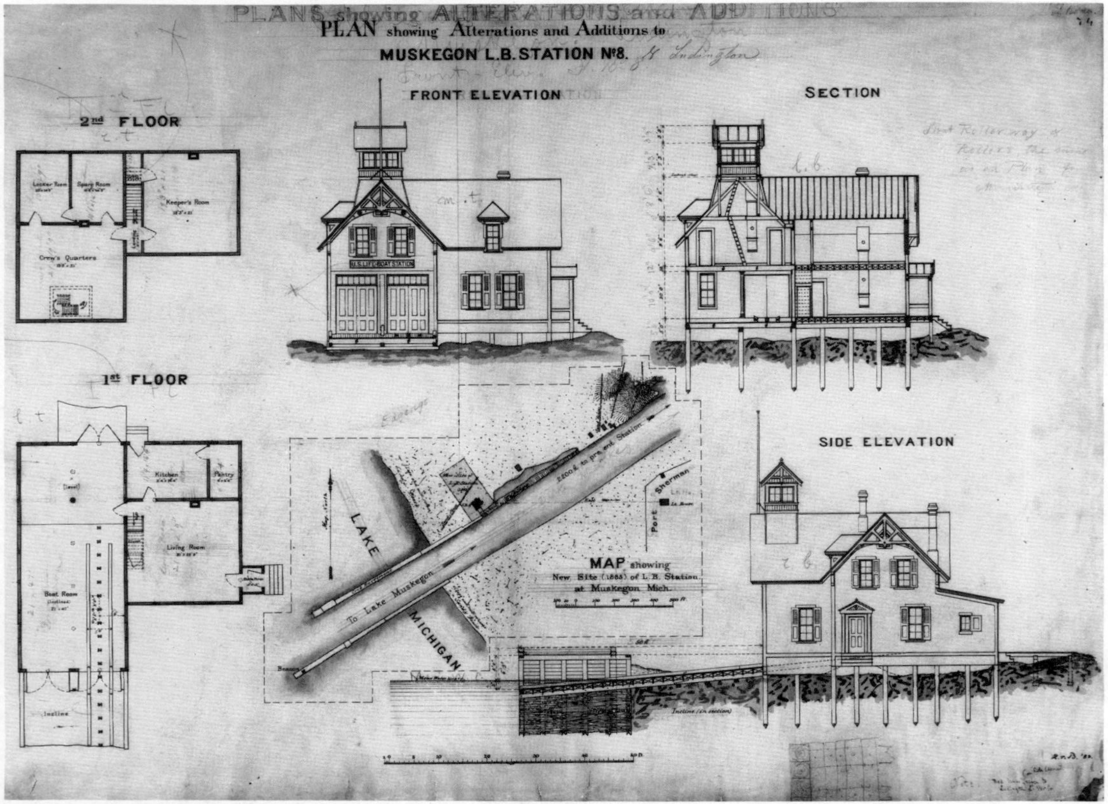

Drawings for station site and building at Muskegon, Michigan. (Center for Cartographic and Architectural Archives, National Archives)

The U.S. Life-Saving Service had two floating stations, one at Louisville, Kentucky, the other at City Point, in Boston Harbor. The rationale for the Louisville Station, the older of the two, lies in the location of a dam and the falls of the Ohio River. A dam was constructed across the falls "with two wide openings or chutes to facilitate the descent of vessels, the ascent being accomplished through a canal provided with locks." The service justified a unit here because "the dam is a source of danger to boats attempting to cross the river to the city of Jeffersonville, as they are liable to be sucked down by the chutes or swept over its verge." Even large steam-powered vessels faced possible danger if they became disabled.[31]

The Louisville Station was placed into commission in 1881 and consisted of a two-story house atop a wooden scow-shaped hull. The house was topped by the inevitable lookout post. The unit had only two "life skiffs" assigned. The houseboat was normally moored in the river above the dam, but could be towed to wherever it was needed in the local area. In 1928 the wooden houseboat was replaced by a steel-hulled craft built in Dubuque, Iowa. The floating station at Louisville was decommissioned in 1964.[32]

Floating station at Louisville, Kentucky. (U.S. Coast Guard)

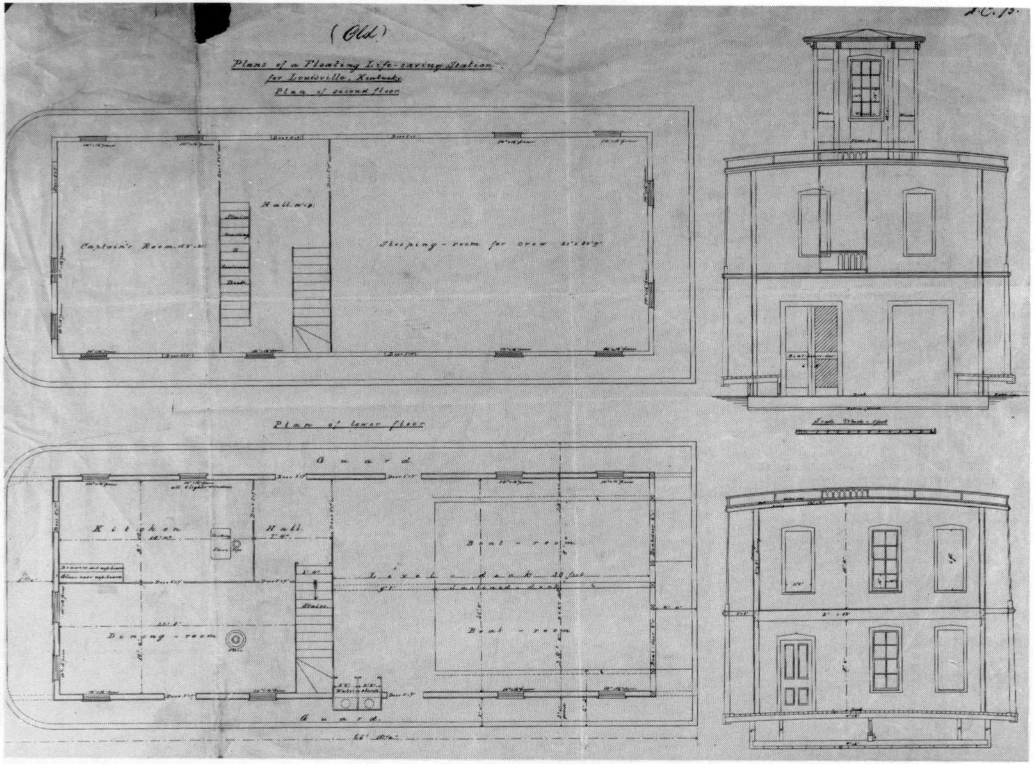

Drawing for the Louisville floating station. (Center for Cartographic and Architectural Archives, National Archives)

Floating station in Boston's harbor. (Mariner's Museum, Newport News, Virginia)

The need for the floating station was graphically demonstrated during the floods of 1883 and 1884. The houseboat was moved from place to place helping those stranded on house roofs. The U.S. Life-Saving Service estimated that during those two years "the crew . . . [of the Louisville Station] rescued and took to places of safety over 800 imperiled . . . men, women, and children . . . and supplied food and other necessities to more than 10,000." In 1899 the keeper of the Louisville Station, Benjamin G. Cameron, was awarded the Silver Life Saving Medal for saving 108 people on "various occasions from 1875 to 1897."[33]

One of the most unusual of all the stations in the U.S. Life-Saving Service deserves mention not for its architecture or its location, but for the makeup of its crew. From 1880 until it was decommissioned in 1947, the Pea Island Station, on the Outer Banks of North Carolina, was crewed entirely by blacks. How could a unit in the nineteenth-century South have such a composition? Its origins can be traced to a shipwreck.

On 30 November 1879, during a period of clear weather, but high seas, the British bark *M & S Henderson* went aground to the south of Pea Island and quickly went to pieces. Surfman Leonidas R. Tillett left the station at around 2:00 A.M. on his south beach patrol, returning about three and a half hours later. After making a fire and calling the cook, he glanced out a window and saw something moving on the beach a long way off. Tillett grabbed a pair of binoculars and saw that it was a man staggering down the beach. Tillett thought the man might be a shipwreck survivor, and he informed Keeper George C. Daniels of the sighting. Daniels, in turn, called out the crew and started down the beach.[34]

The man turned out to be a survivor of the *M & S Henderson.* He was so exhausted and confused he could only manage to mutter: "Captain drowned, mast gone." Daniels detailed Tillett to help the sailor back to the station. Then, according to the keeper's sworn statement, the crew pushed on, lugging the station's medicine chest. Tillett escorted the sailor to the unit and left him in care of the "colored . . . female cook" and set out to catch up with Daniels. The lifesavers in the meantime arrived at New Inlet, where they were met by a party of fishermen who informed the rescue party that they had found a man floating in the channel and taken him to a camp. On the way to the camp, the lifesavers found another survivor and helped him to the location of his shipmate. Then Daniels administered stimulants to the two shipwrecked sailors.

The officer assigned to investigate the wreck, 1st Lt. Charles F. Shoemaker, arrived at Pea Island in January 1880. Shoemaker questioned why Surfman Tillett, whose patrol should have taken him by the wreck site, had not spotted the *M & S Henderson.* After a number of interviews, the inspector concluded that because the night was exceptionally fine, the surfman was "intent only upon getting back to the station" and had not "kept a bright lookout." Tillett's "failure to do so . . . is . . . the neglect of the most important duty of a patrolman."

Shoemaker then turned his attention to Keeper Daniels's sworn statement. After questioning a number of witnesses and confronting the keeper, the inspector learned that the keeper had lied about bringing the medicine chest with him and, in fact, had had to send a surfman back to retrieve it. Shoemaker recommended the dismissal of Daniels, for lying under oath, and the removal of Tillett, for neglect of duty, and one other surfman. In short, half the station's crew was dismissed. Then Lt. Charles F. Shoemaker penned the following: "I recommend Richard Etheridge, colored," to be keeper of Pea Island.

Etheridge, according to Shoemaker, was "thirty-eight years of age, [of] strong robust physique, intelligent, and able to read and write sufficiently well to keep the journal of a station." The officer also noted that the selectee was "one of the best surfmen on this part of the coast of North Carolina." Realizing the difficulties inherent in a black man commanding a white crew, Shoemaker recommended the crew be entirely black, by retaining two black surfmen already serving at the station, transferring two other blacks from another station, and allowing Etheridge to select two additional men. The white men would be trans-

Pea Island, North Carolina, the only unit in the history of the service to be crewed solely by African-Americans; Richard Etheridge, first African-American keeper, is at far left. (Outer Banks History Center, Manteo, North Carolina)

ferred to another unit. In a fine piece of understatement, Shoemaker informed headquarters that he was "aware that no colored man holds the position of Keeper in the Life-Saving Service, and yet such as are surfmen, are found to be among the best on the coast of North Carolina."

Why did Lieutenant Shoemaker make what for that time and place was a radical recommendation? There is nothing to show his reasoning. Perhaps he was simply color-blind in matters of the service. Shoemaker wrote that he had "given this matter as careful consideration as I am capable of and have tried to weigh every argument, for and against its adoption, and I am fully convinced that the efficiency of the service at this station, will be greatly enhanced by the adoption of my recommendation." Subsequent events proved the wisdom of his decision.

Soon after Etheridge began his duties, the station burned down. The service never laid the blame for the incident on anyone, probably reasoning that to accuse any local resident would cause even more discontent.

But a guard was assigned to watch the lumber for a new building to be erected on the site of the former station. Eventually, the crew was accepted. Etheridge clearly demonstrated his abilities on 11 October 1896.[35]

On that evening the schooner *E. S. Newman* found herself battling the strong winds and seas of a hurricane. The winds soon tore the *Newman*'s sails to ribbons and her skipper decided to beach her. The schooner came to rest some two miles below the Pea Island Station and the captain shot off distress signals. The beach patrol from the lifesaving station fired off his Coston signal to inform the shipwrecked sailors that help would be on the way and then hurried back to the station to give the alarm. Keeper Etheridge and his crew started to the scene with the beach apparatus.[36]

The hurricane's strength drove the seas to such a height that they were "sweeping over the beach and threatened to prevent" the lifesavers from reaching the scene of the wreck. Somehow the Pea Island crew managed to reach the site, but found the beach so flooded that it was impossible to set up their equipment. Keeper Etheridge then hit upon a bold plan. He had two surfmen tie a stout line to themselves and see how close to the wreck they could get. One can only imagine what the two surfmen thought as they set out into the dark night to fight their way into the pounding surf. With great effort the lifesavers managed to get close enough to heave a line to the schooner. The crew of the *Newman* realized that their only hope of rescue was to be pulled through the surf by the men in oilskins. The first survivor pulled from the sea was the three-year-old child of the captain; the next person was the skipper's wife. Eventually the remaining seven crew members were pulled by rope through the waves by the black lifesavers from the Pea Island Station.

Halfway across the continent from Pea Island, at Evanston, Illinois, was another station with an unusual crew. The station was located on the grounds of Northwestern University and the surfmen were made up largely of students. In 1890 the entire crew won the Gold Life Saving Medal for a daring rescue in which they pushed out into a November storm and, although completely coated in ice, saved the crew from the steamer *Calumet*.[37]

Once Kimball had organized the service, provided for the expansion of the organization, and established a personnel system, he faced two major battles on behalf of the lifesavers. One campaign centered on pay; the other dealt with obtaining a retirement and disability system for the lifesavers. The issue of pay was an ongoing battle, and salaries increased with all the speed of a glacier. In 1878 the salary of a keeper was two

Station at Evansville, Illinois, on the grounds of Northwestern University, was crewed by students. V-shaped pole was used for practice with beach apparatus. (U.S. Coast Guard)

hundred dollars a year. By 1892 a keeper's wages were nine hundred dollars per year and this salary remained the same until the service was incorporated into the coast guard. Surfmen's wages made the same slow progress. Crewmen at first earned ten dollars for each rescue they actually performed. They were not paid for the hours of drill and other duties. This inequity was rectified in 1871; the men then received fifty dollars a month regardless of their ranking in the crew. In 1882 pay was increased another ten dollars. By 1914 a surfman still earned only sixty dollars per month during the active season.[38]

Two important changes made matters worse. On 3 August 1894 the active season on the East Coast was expanded to include the period from 1 August to 1 June.[39] Previously, a fisherman on the eastern seaboard could serve in the U.S. Life-Saving Service during the slack fishing season. In fact the service provided a good second job for fishermen. With the extended active season, however, crewmen were now forced to decide whether to stay with the U.S. Life-Saving Service or continue fishing and seek other employment during the slack season. Many decided on the latter course of action.[40]

The other major change occurred as Americans began to view the seashore as a place of recreation. Prior to the mid-nineteenth century few people in the United States considered the beach as a recreational area. The growing interest in the coastal region as a place of leisure and play offered a new source of income for watermen, either full time or as a means to augment their income during breaks from commercial fishing. As the pay for keepers and surfmen stagnated, many men realized they could fish for part of the year, cater to the tourist trade for the remainder of the year, and still make more money than by serving in the U.S. Life-Saving Service.

The importance of pay cannot be overlooked. Of the 1,902 surfmen who served on Lake Michigan from 1871 to 1913, 1 percent gave low pay as the reason for leaving the service. Another 28 percent left seeking "other business," a possible indication that pay was not sufficient. Kimball recognized the importance of good wages, but was only partially successful in obtaining adequate pay for his lifesavers.[41]

Even more important was Kimball's campaign for a retirement and disability system. If a lifesaver was injured or killed in the line of duty there was no system to compensate him or his widow and children. In 1882 a limited system was put into force, whereby a widow would receive one year's pay for a death in the line of duty. This was the extent of the benefits. From 1876 until 1914 Kimball lobbied unsuccessfully for a retirement and disability system. The mandatory yearly physical examinations instituted in the 1880s increased the need for a retirement or compensation system. Lifesavers worked in all kinds of weather, with the real chance of injury or death. A keeper might serve honorably and bravely for many years, only to be forced to resign without compensation because of injuries or the natural infirmities of advancing age.

Theoretically a keeper could remain on duty for his entire life, if he could pass the annual physical. At the age of seventy-five the legendary Joshua James, keeper of the station at Point Allerton, Massachusetts, made what would be his last trip in a boat. He stepped ashore and died. Without a retirement system promotions to keeper also stagnated. The men in charge, who should have been young enough to take the punishment of small boat operations, grew old in the service. The lack of a retirement system also was unfair to those who served for many years only to be turned out when they grew too old.[42]

Kimball was successful in many of his undertakings concerning the U.S. Life-Saving Service, but he was notably unsuccessful in his efforts to obtain a retirement system. The specific reasons for this failure are difficult to pin down. The simplistic answer is a parsimonious Congress. This is almost certainly not the only answer. The service was largely a part-time organization; most of its employees, the surfmen, worked no more than ten months a year. This undoubtedly increased the difficulty of selling the idea of a retirement system to Congress. If a single reason must be given, it was probably that government, reflecting the attitudes of the times, simply was not yet ready to award retirement money for nonmilitary service, no matter how worthy the organization.

By the late 1880s the service was well established and it would have been politically unwise for any congressman to argue against an organization that saved countless numbers of lives. And Kimball generally enjoyed a reputation many in the Washington establishment might have envied; nevertheless some grumblings about the man were heard. One detractor noted that Kimball was one of those who "gets himself picked as one of the *indispensables* that the Govmt [*sic*] cannot get along without." In 1913 an anonymous writer stated that Kimball was seventy-nine and not "well preserved." He "constantly besieges Congress continually for . . . retirement, with pay, for himself." The writer accused Kimball of forcing keepers and surfmen to contribute money for a campaign to obtain such a law. He also stated that Kimball's crews were made up of "men of limited education and experience, easily the prey of the unscrupulous" and had looked to Kimball to guard their interests, but instead he took their money for a fund to promote retirement. Kimball's rebuttal to the secretary of the treasury included a comment that he felt he was "pretty well preserved," having been out of the office for only two periods of more than ten days in the last thirty years. In defending his men the general superintendent said that although some surfmen may "possess limited education," keepers were well qualified for any clerical work that their position required.

A delegation of New Jersey Democrats in the House of Representatives, upon learning about a keeper from New Jersey who had been dismissed by Kimball, cited reasons for the removal of the general superintendent, the strongest being he was "an unscrupulous and pernicious partisan, . . . a keen and adroit politician whose exertions are ever in the interest of Republican principles." Further, the delegation wrote that the claim that the office of general superintendent was nonpartisan "cannot be sustained. The life-saving forces have at all times been religiously used in the cutting down of Democratic majorities."[43]

The above comments are the strongest complaints I have seen laid against Kimball in my nearly twenty years of research on the U.S. Life-

Saving Service. For a man who for more than forty years was the head of a very visible organization in politically charged Washington, D.C., Kimball's reputation remains amazingly unsullied. Leonard D. White writes that Kimball, along with a few other men in government service during the period from 1869 to 1901, was one of the "most trustworthy public officials in the history of the Republic"; such men "of quality . . . became the prevalent type . . . , and by the end of the century the public had come to expect decency and honor in the executive branch."[44]

Sumner Increase Kimball is the towering figure in the history of the U.S. Life-Saving Service. During a seven-year span beginning in 1871, he promulgated a set of regulations, established a personnel system, and provided a means to expand the organization in a logical and orderly manner. The operational procedures he set into motion lasted well into the U.S. Coast Guard era. Some can still be seen today. His greatest failure was his inability to obtain a retirement system for his lifesavers. Perhaps the real genius of Kimball is that when he found himself in charge of a loosely organized network of lifesaving stations, he recognized that the concept of shore-based lifesaving had the potential for great expansion. He understood that the only way this expansion could succeed was under a tight, centrally controlled organization of national scope. To this end, he applied his talents to bring the units under federal control. Very early in the process he recognized the dramatic value of his field units and was quick to use what we would now call the power of the media to help him attain his goal. By employing the writer William D. O'Connor as his assistant Kimball was able to make the U.S. Life-Saving Service "as popular as the U.S. Cavalry" in the public's mind.[45]

CHAPTER FOUR

Just the U.S. Government's Hired Man: The Men of the U.S. Life-Saving Service

The men who served at the small rescue stations that dotted America's coastline were the heart of the U.S. Life-Saving Service. Some of the rescues performed by the lifesavers were indeed remarkable, and the press soon began to describe crewmen in such colorful terms as "storm warriors" and "soldiers of the surf." Despite their importance, their bravery, and the publicity they received, very little is known about the individuals who served. Instead, a myth that began in the nineteenth century continues to be perpetuated. The usual version describes the keeper as someone who had years of experience in a maritime trade, usually fishing; he had little formal education, but was honest and adept at handling men and boats. And he had spent many years at one station, thus becoming an expert on his area of operations. Part of the reason for the myth is the good public relations promoted by Sumner I. Kimball and William D. O'Connor. The press would receive the written exploits of exciting rescues released by Kimball and O'Connor, then add their own colorful descriptions. The crewmen quickly became larger than life. Most reporters failed to obtain biographical information on the lifesavers.

Another important reason for a lack of in-depth studies on crewmen is the poor personnel records maintained by the U.S. Life-Saving Service. Instead of service jackets, personnel data were entered into handwritten journals. A few entries are relatively complete, but most contain only minimal information. When the organization came under civil service rules, keepers filed letters of application giving some information on their lives. Not all of these letters are extant, however. Only two studies have been made on those who served in the U.S. Life-Saving Service, and these were for only a few stations in a limited area, such as along Cape Cod.[1] To provide a better understanding of the men who served in the U.S. Life-Saving Service, this chapter discusses the men in general, then focuses on one U.S. Life-Saving Service District, the Eleventh, which encompassed Lake Michigan. The personnel records at this district are relatively complete. Information will deal primarily with the keepers as data are almost nonexistent for surfmen.

The official title for the man in charge of the station, keeper, comes from the volunteer era, when one man remained at a station and was responsible for watching over—or keeping—the unit and its equipment. The service officially designated keeper as the title for the man in charge, but the local community and crew always referred to him as captain. And the keeper had, in fact, all the power of a seagoing skipper.

The log books of the service are replete with entries like "Launched lifeboat, saved 11 people," with no further details.[2] These terse recordings may indicate that writing was not the keepers' forte, or perhaps the men were simply laconic. Some keepers were able to express themselves quite well, if not eloquently, in writing. Keeper Thomas Matthews, of the station at Point Betsie, Michigan, wrote such a detailed log on the wreck of the *J. H. Hartzell* that his entries were the basis for a video production depicting the incident.[3] I believe the short journal entries can be explained by a combination of natural taciturnity and a feeling that no matter how difficult the rescue, the lifesavers were simply doing their duty. Most of the crews believed in the traditional sailor's effort to help another sailor in distress. The service's obsession with thrift may also have contributed to short journal entries. As Nell Wise Wechter points out, the organization supplied very little paper and issued only a pint of ink, "which probably outlasted the life of the station. There was an occasional lead pencil and, quadrennially, pens and pen staffs would arrive." A keeper was expected not to waste paper on unnecessary comments.[4]

Most keepers had a reputation for being tough and capable of handling rough, hard-to-manage crews. In some cases the rank and file did not take kindly to authority. In 1876 a visitor to the isolated stations along the coast of Lake Superior reported that Keeper Quinton Morgan's crew of the unit at Sucker River, Michigan, consisted of loggers who did not appreciate Morgan's discipline and were fast approaching mutiny. The keeper claimed that a crewman had already jumped him one night as he walked the beach. Morgan swore the men intended to hang him. To foil this alleged plot, the keeper carried a revolver in his shirt and kept a hatchet beside him in the stern of the boat whenever he took his crew out into the lake.[5]

Most keepers did not have to resort to Morgan's tactics to enforce their authority. The men in charge of stations were generally well known, respected boatmen in the communities where the units were located. Most of the crewmen were from the same communities and familiar with the keeper's reputation. It is perhaps important to note that most crewmen were watermen and knew that a small boat in the raging surf was no place for a democratic discussion. They understood that only one man could be in charge. This does not mean there were no incompetent keepers, nor ones that crewmen did not respect.

Most of the keepers came from humble means. Many of the service's stations were located in regions that we would label as "economically depressed." One applicant for a keeper's vacancy along the Outer Banks of North Carolina wrote that he was "a poor man" and needed the position. When scanning the personnel lists for the remote stations, a researcher is struck by another feature concerning the crewmen: the large family groups on the rolls. For example, along the Outer Banks of North Carolina, Greys, Stowes, Ethridges, and Scarboroughs show up with regularity. The Midgetts, however, are probably more represented than any other family. Members of this family have served in the U.S. Coast Guard and its predecessors since at least 1874. One Midgett observed that on the Outer Banks "you could either sit around and fish, or you could go out and save lives" and the family chose the latter.[6] Regulations stated that keepers were not to employ members of their family, but in isolated regions this regulation was not always strictly observed. A case in point occurred near the station at Gull Shoal, North Carolina. A keeper wrote to the superintendent of the Sixth District that Gull Shoal was commanded by J. B. Midgett. J. M. Midgett was his brother-in-law, E. Midgett married the keeper's sister, B. Midgett married the keeper's wife's daughter, and D. Lowry was the keeper's brother-in-law. The remaining two men at the station, according to the informant, could also be related to the keeper. It is not clear whether this report was sent to the superintendent because of the breach of regulations or because of family jealousy.[7]

One part of the myth that has been perpetuated about keepers is their length of service. Keeper John D. Persons, of the station at Thunder Bay Island, Michigan, began his career on 15 January 1878 and was still in command in 1915.[8] Keeper Jarvis B. Rider began his tenure at the station at Little Egg, New Jersey, on 3 November 1869, during the volunteer era. Forty-six years later Jarvis was still in command of the same unit, giving him the distinction of having the longest continuous tenure in the history of the service. Rider once remarked that he had never served as a surfman but entered the volunteer organization at age twenty. He was one of twenty-one children, seven of whom lived to adulthood. His father, Ebner Rider, was a lighthouse keeper at Tucker's Beach, New Jersey. Four of Jarvis's brothers served either in the U.S. Life-Saving

Keeper John D. Persons (far right), longest continuous-serving keeper on the Great Lakes. Keepers' coats were double-breasted. Surfmen wore their rank number on the left sleeve, with eight being the most junior. Lifeboat stations usually had eight men, lifesaving stations six. (From the Jesse Besser Museum Collection, Alpena, Michigan)

Crew of the station at Kitty Hawk, North Carolina. Crewmen wore the service's logo (life buoy and crossed boat hooks) on the right sleeve; keepers' hats had a pin with the logo. The keeper (3d from right) has been identified as Samuel J. Payne. (U.S. Coast Guard)

Service or the U.S. Lighthouse Service. Keepers John Persons and Jarvis Rider seem to confirm the myth of long-serving keepers.[9] But an examination of the personnel rolls of the service disputes this conclusion (see table 1).

In the Great Lakes region, only 15 percent of the men served more than twenty years. The average length of service in that region is only eight years. This is a far cry from the long-service keeper of legend. The personnel records of the U.S. Life-Saving Service indicate that more than half the keepers left the service for nondisciplinary reasons (see table 2).[10] Thirty percent resigned. Factors such as few pay increases, no retirement benefits, and very little compensation in case of duty-related injury are reflected in the information presented in table 2. Physical health was the second highest reason for nondisciplinary resignations from the service. Although personnel records sometimes stated "resigned," keepers were often forced to leave their positions because of health.

Though the U.S. Life-Saving Service's personnel records are spotty, I believe we can safely infer that many keepers left due to poor wages. The Golden Gate Station, located in San Francisco's Golden Gate Park, can hardly be called an isolated station. The first keeper was assigned to this unit on 2 August 1878. Over the next thirty-seven years eleven keepers served at the unit. One keeper became district superintendent,

TABLE 4.1
Keepers in Long Service, By Region, 1871(?)–1913(?)

REGION[a]	20–30 YEARS (%)	30+ YEARS (%)	STATISTICAL AVERAGE[b] (YEARS)
Great Lakes	15	4	8
West Coast	10	—	7
Northeast	10	3	9
Middle Atlantic	11	2	9
Southeast	18	10	9
Gulf	5	—	6

SOURCE: Register of Employees, U.S. Life-Saving Service, 1871(?)–1913(?), Records of the U.S. Coast Guard, RG26, National Archives, Washington, D.C.

NOTE: $N = 711$. The total number of keepers who served in the U.S. Life-Saving Service was 984. After factoring out those still serving in 1915, and thus officially in the U.S. Coast Guard, the total was 711.

[a] The regions follow the U.S. Life-Saving Service's districts. Great Lakes: all states encompassed by the Great Lakes, plus one station in Ky.; West Coast: Alaska, Calif., Ore., Wash.; Northeast: Conn., Mass., Maine, N.H., R.I.; Middle Atlantic: coastal areas of Del., N.J., N.Y.; Southeast: Md., N.C., Va.; Gulf: Fla., Tex.

[b] In computing the statistical average, those who served one year or less or more than twenty years were discarded.

one transferred, one resigned due to "ill health," and another keeper's "services" were "discontinued." The remaining seven men are logged as simply "resigned." The average length of service of the seven men who resigned was two years. This unit was located in an urban area, and the opportunity for better employment may have been a significant factor in why so many keepers resigned. This may also have been true in other units.

The isolation of many stations may well have been another reason keepers left the service. The station at Cape Aargo, Oregon, a rather isolated unit near the California-Oregon border, saw its first keeper assigned in 1878. Thirty-seven years later fourteen keepers had held command at this station. This is the largest turnover for any unit on the West Coast. Of the fourteen men who served at Cape Aargo four transferred to other stations; the others resigned. The undesirability of the station is implicit in the account of Martin Jacobson. In 1900 he was willing to take a reduction to surfman to transfer to the station at Shoalwater Bay, Washington. I could find only one other keeper in the history of the U.S. Life-Saving Service who did this. (Of course Jacobson

TABLE 4.2
Profile of Keepers: Nationally, 1871(?)–1913(?)

REASON FOR LEAVING POSITION (%)		
Nondisciplinary		
Resigned	30	
Physical Health	11	
Death[a]	9	
Other	3	
Total[b]		53
Disciplinary		15
Unknown		33
LENGTH OF SERVICE (%)		
20–30 years	13	
30+ years	2	
STATISTICAL AVERAGE[c]: 8 YEARS		

SOURCE: Register of Employees, U.S. Life-Saving Service, 1871(?)–1913(?), Records of the U.S. Coast Guard, Record Group 26, National Archives, Washington, D.C.
NOTE: $N = 711$.
[a] 10 men drowned; 57 died from unknown causes.
[b] Totals do not add to 100 percent because of missing data.
[c] The statistical average was computed by ignoring less than one year or more than twenty years of service.

may simply have wished to move.) Although keepers undoubtedly resigned from the service for other reasons as well, low pay, no retirement, and isolation must be considered the primary causes.

In the Eleventh U.S. Life-Saving District, along the shores of Lake Michigan, most keepers brought substantial experience to their positions. Of the thirty-four letters of application still extant, one keeper had twenty-four years of experience and eleven had ten or more. The least experience was only two years, but it was in the U.S. Life-Saving Service. The men brought an average of eight and a half years of maritime service to their positions.

One thirty-two-year-old man claimed he had sailed since the age of fifteen. Another, at the age of twenty-six, claimed he was accustomed to boating "all my lifetime." A forty-one-year-old salt wrote that he had sailed for twenty-four years, been a mate and master, and had assisted in a rescue with a Francis metallic lifeboat. Another forty-year-old applicant stated he had ten years of U.S. Life-Saving Service experience, plus additional time sailing both "before the mast" (as a regular sailor) and as an officer. One rather honest twenty-eight-year-old applicant stated that he had entered the service with very little experience, but after eight years of work he had "got confidence in my self [*sic*] about handling a boat." In short, the keepers on Lake Michigan substantiate the myth that keepers had years of maritime experience.

Of the 121 keepers who served on Lake Michigan, 40 percent were foreign born, with most from Canada and the Scandinavian countries (see table 3). The average age of a keeper at the time of his appointment was 38.8 years, with the oldest being 69 and the youngest 26.

Two interesting statistics indicate that the myth of long service at one station needs to be reexamined. More than three-quarters of the keepers left their units after serving no more than ten years, with 33 percent leaving after only two years or less. Forty percent of the keepers in the district were transferred at least one time. In many cases the men were seeking less isolated stations or they seemed not to fit into the local community.

On 8 June 1897, Charles Tufts, commanding the station at Ludington, Michigan, wrote to the superintendent of the district that he had "some kind of . . . asthma trouble" and any exertion would set him "to wheezing." Tufts had thought over the matter of resignation for a year. He stated he would have resigned earlier, but debts forced him to remain. Tufts went on to say that he did not "want any one to lose there [*sic*] lives or run any chances on account of my health." Tufts knew that he was not in any "condition to stand what a Keeper of a station should be able to stand." He had "been hanging on for the last year to see if there would not be some kind of a Pension law passed that would strike my case." Rather poignantly, the keeper noted that he had seventeen years of service and did not want "the station or service to be found fault with in any way on my account." Tufts wished to be carried on a pension list and wanted to know if the superintendent felt there was a chance to receive one. In closing, Tufts wrote "I have done my best for the Service while I have been in it and I hope they will do there [*sic*] best by me." Kimball's endorsement to the secretary of the treasury was a laconic recommendation that the resignation of Keeper Tufts be accepted "to take effect immediately." Similar letters are scattered throughout the files of the U.S. Life-Saving Service.

A number of the men in charge of lifesaving stations along Lake Michigan were dismissed from the service. The specter of men drinking to excess, a common affliction of sailors, haunted the U.S. Life-Saving

TABLE 4.3
Profile of Keepers: Lake Michigan, 1871(?)–1913(?)

PLACE OF BIRTH[a]	(%)
In-state (Unit Site)	31
Out-of-state	26
Foreign	40
AVERAGE AGE AT APPOINTMENT: 38.8 YEARS	
LENGTH OF SERVICE	**(%)**
Years	
Less than 1	16
1–2	17
3–5	22
6–10	24
11–15	8
16–20	7
21+	6
REASON FOR LEAVING SERVICE	**(%)**
Resigned	14
Resigned (for physical reason)	4
Death	4
Drowned	2
Discharged	2
Dispensed with Services	2
Removed	2
Revoked	1
Promoted to Superintendent	[1 man]
Still serving (in 1913)	24
Transferred	40

SOURCE: Register of Employees, U.S. Life-Saving Service, 1871(?)–1913(?), Records of the U.S. Coast Guard, RG26, National Archives, Washington, D.C.
NOTE: $N = 121$
[a] Totals do not add to 100 percent because of missing data.

Service. A headline screaming Lives Lost Because of Drunken Lifesavers was the last thing Kimball wished to see. In most endorsements recommending a man for keeper, the superintendent of the district noted the applicant's temperate habits. In spite of a fairly vigorous program to weed out drunkards, from time to time keepers were removed for excessive use of alcohol. Capt. Thomas Walker, chief inspector of the U.S. Life-Saving Service, in dismissing an Eleventh District keeper for drinking, stated that even though the man had been in the service "upwards of fifteen years, and over one-third of this time as keeper," and was "a very good boatman, . . . the business of saving life and property" demanded "sober men and the Service [could not] afford to temporize" on sobriety among its keepers. Another keeper was removed for drinking, plus four additional charges. Among the "rascalities of the Keeper" was theft of raspberries, fishing nets, and other items.

One keeper in Michigan ran into problems when he tried to dismiss two crewmen. The men, in turn, filed charges against the keeper for running a "boat livery" from the station and, even more serious, for making false journal entries. The assistant inspector of the district, Nathaniel Robbins, thought the problems stemmed from the keeper being "a very nice easygoing man, and no doubt but the men take more or less advantage of his good nature." Apparently, this "easygoing" nature and the two charges were enough to cause Kimball to write that the keeper's resignation would be accepted "if tendered immediately." Another inspector in the Eleventh District reported that a keeper was a "coward" and appeared "to be afraid of his crew." According to the report the man had reached his position "by accident," as he was serving at a station when his predecessor died and the "coward" was the crewman with the most experience.

A Wisconsin keeper was bold enough to threaten the assistant inspector and to imply a threat to the district superintendent upon hearing a rumor that he might be replaced. The keeper stated that he would "make things very interesting for [the assistant inspector] in the Service." The district superintendent noted that any "insinuations only show a weakness in the upper story." Not too surprisingly, the keeper was removed from the service. Yet another man was removed for alleged bigamy.

Obviously not every keeper in the Eleventh District was the highly respected man of myth. Just as obviously not all keepers were immoral, were drunkards, or had a touch of larceny. Only 7 percent of the men in charge of the Eleventh District's stations were dismissed. The great majority of keepers did not blemish the image of the service. An examination of the lifesavers serving along Lake Michigan's shoreline reveals a diverse, interesting group of individuals rather than the rather homogeneous hero of legend. To be sure, there were heroes serving within the district. Keeper Lawrence O. Lawson, of the station at Evanston, Illinois, winner of the Gold Life Saving Medal, was an expert on handling boats and men and can deservedly be called a hero. At the other end of the spectrum were the keepers who were dismissed for bigamy, drunkenness, or "rascalities." The majority of men who served as keepers in the U.S. Life-Saving Service on Lake Michigan fall between these two extremes. Using information from application forms and the personnel journals, we can compose a biographical sketch of the "average" keeper who served within the Eleventh U.S. Life-Saving District from 1871 to 1915.

He was almost thirty-nine years of age at his appointment and brought several years of maritime experience to his position. This experience might include service in the U.S. Life-Saving Service, on ships, or in other related maritime activities, but was most likely to be fishing. Our average keeper spent no more than ten years in the U.S. Life-Saving Service, and during this time he was likely to be transferred. The keeper probably left the service for better pay.

Information on keepers is sparse, and data on the rank and file, the surfmen, is almost nonexistent. Except on the West Coast, surfmen were employed only part-time, during the active season when shipwrecks were

Crew of Big Sandy, on Lake Ontario, with a uniform of their own, complete with derby hat. One of the earliest stations in the Great Lakes, it had open lookout platforms and walkway on roof. (U.S. Coast Guard)

Unidentified crew with their unusual uniforms may be from Big Sandy; rank numbers are on belts. (U.S. Coast Guard)

most likely to occur. The men signed articles of agreement to work for a stipulated period of time, and the only information on the men comes from the very sparse data entered into the personnel rolls and the few references found in keepers' letters. The myth of the surfman closely parallels that of the keeper: a waterman with many years of experience, who spends many years at a station, advances slowly, and eventually is promoted to keeper. One surfman will serve as representative for all the forgotten men who filled the ranks of the service.

Theodore Roberge was born in Crookston, Minnesota, in 1889, the youngest of thirteen children. His father was a police officer in St. Paul. Part of the Roberge family moved to Seattle, Washington, where Theodore entered the U.S. Navy as an enlisted man at the age of sixteen. He served for one enlistment on the Yangtze River patrol in China. He then returned to Seattle to work as a tinsmith. After serving as a coxswain for one enlistment in the U.S. Revenue Cutter Service, Roberge entered the U.S. Life-Saving Service in 1911.[11] Roberge's first duty station in the U.S. Life-Saving Service was at Cape Disappointment, Washington. This unit, just north of the Columbia River, is noted for being near some

Crew at Neah Bay, Washington, 1910. (Coast Guard Museum Northwest)

of the highest surf in the United States. Within two years of signing on, Roberge was involved in the heroic rescue attempt of the crew of the tanker *Rosecrans*.[12]

On 4 January 1913 the *Rosecrans* left Monterey, California, with nineteen thousand barrels of crude oil bound for Portland, Oregon. In the early morning hours of 7 January the tanker was approaching the Columbia River in thick fog and heavy winds. The *Rosecrans* struck heavily on Peacock Spit near the entrance to the Columbia River; later investigation concluded that an error had been made in navigation. A ship grounding on the spit was "either quickly pounded to pieces by the terrific breakers or swallowed up by yielding quicksands." On the morning of 7 January the surf was extremely heavy. When the tanker struck, the skipper managed to get out one wireless distress message. The operator who received the message sent out a general distress message, but got no response. He then called a tug company's office and asked them to contact the U.S. Life-Saving Service stations at Point Adams, Oregon, and Cape Disappointment, Washington. The telephone lines were out of order to Cape Disappointment, but the message was relayed to Point Adams. Three and a half hours after the tanker had grounded, the lookout tower watch at Cape Disappointment spotted the *Rosecrans*. Keeper Alfred Rimer went to the tower and, even though no distress flags were flying, he decided to push out in the station's power lifeboat. Rimer and his crew had no way of knowing that thirty-two of the thirty-six crew members had already drowned, swept off the tanker shortly after she stranded.

The lifeboat hit the full fury of the seas and was forced back. The seas were estimated to be at least forty feet. Keeper Rimer tried another tack and was again forced back. Before his next attempt, he spotted a tug and asked to be towed across the bar, but the skipper did not want to risk the fury of the seas. Once again the lifeboat made the attempt, only to be driven back.

Meanwhile Keeper Oscar S. Wicklund and the crew of the Point Adams Station set out to find the wreck. Unable to locate the ship, the keeper decided to cross the Columbia River to confer with the Cape Disappointment Station. Once the two keepers got together, Keeper Wicklund decided he would try to reach the ship. By this time, three men could be seen clinging to the rigging of the *Rosecrans*. Keeper Wicklund later said that he did not "have much hope of reaching the vessel, but I thought it would encourage those men in the rigging if they saw the lifeboat constantly trying to reach them." The boat made two attempts and once the craft was "entirely submerged." Again, the lifesavers returned to shelter. In the best tradition of the U.S. Life-Saving Service, Keepers Rimer and Wicklund decided that they "would not quit trying as long as there was anyone left in the rigging."

The next attempt was made by both boats, with the Cape Disappointment crew leading the way. This time they managed to get close enough to signal the sailors in the rigging to jump. Keeper Wicklund then noticed the Cape Disappointment boat seemed to be in trouble. Keeper Rimer's boat had capsized and the motor had been damaged. The crew then broke out the oars, even though they saw that the boat's bottom was damaged. In the meantime the Point Adams boat continued to circle and try to coax the *Rosecrans* sailors into the water. On the beginning of its fifth circuit around the tanker, the lifeboat was struck by "a terrific sea" and she turned turtle, throwing the crew into the sea. Everyone except Surfman Pearson managed to grab the boat's rail. When the boat righted itself, the crew scrambled into the boat and spotted Pearson drifting about three hundred yards away. The lifesavers got Pearson aboard; then they realized that the Cape Disappointment crew was signaling for help. The boat was safely pulled in by the Point Adams crew.

Keeper Wicklund's crew pushed out again into the towering seas. This time two of the sailors leaped into the water and were picked up. The other sailor appeared to be dead; he fell to the deck and was washed over the side. The body was recovered. Keeper Wicklund did not think he could get back safely across the bar, so he set course for the open sea to where the Columbia River Lightship was moored. It took approximately three hours to reach the lightship. The lifeboat could not be hoisted aboard, and during the night it broke its line and was lost. The Cape

Disappointment boat was also lost when being towed by a tug. The third survivor of the *Rosecrans* managed to reach shore by clinging to a piece of driftwood.

Although most of the crew aboard the *Rosecrans* perished, the efforts of the lifesavers were commendable. The official report of the incident noted that both crews worked against "distressing odds" and exhibited an "indomitable spirit." Considering the state of the sea, it seemed "little short of miraculous that . . . all [of the lifesavers] escaped with their lives." The legislature of Oregon adopted a resolution commending the lifesavers of both stations and both crews received the Gold Life Saving Medal for their efforts.

Based on the statistics for the surfmen who served along Lake Michigan, the mythic image of the rank and file must also be reconsidered. Of the 1,902 surfmen who served from 1876 to 1913, 69 percent were from the United States (see table 4). Interestingly enough, although the regulations stated that keepers were to hire local boatmen, 31 percent of the men were born in a different community from the one they were serving in. (Of course the men may have moved from their original birthplaces to the locations where they were hired.) Most of the foreign-born serving on Lake Michigan came from the Scandinavian countries and Canada.[13]

The average age of a surfman was twenty-seven. The youngest to be hired during this period was eighteen and the oldest fifty-four. The men who served on Lake Michigan had fishing and other maritime experience. One occupation registered in the personnel rolls for Lake Michigan that is not found on the East Coast was raftman. When the lumber industry was booming in Michigan many of the logs were floated down rivers in large rafts to mills. The raftmen would ride the logs to prevent them from jamming in the river.

Some of the most interesting data reflected in table 4 concern length of service and reasons for leaving the service. Completely breaking the stereotypical image of the long-serving surfman, 37 percent of the rank and file left the service after less than one year of service; 28 percent left within two years. In other words, 65 percent of the surfmen left within two years of signing on. Twenty-eight percent of the men left because of "other business." Although only 1 percent of the lifesavers gave "pay" as the reason for leaving, I believe that "other business" might be read as a euphemism for "better pay."

The largest turnovers in personnel came primarily at stations located near larger communities or urban areas. Chicago, for example, had a

TABLE 4.4
Profile of Surfmen: Lake Michigan, 1871(?)–1913(?)

PLACE OF BIRTH	(%)
In-state (unit site)	31
Out-of-state	40
Foreign	29

AVERAGE AGE AT ENLISTMENT: 27 YEARS

LENGTH OF SERVICE[a]	(%)
Years	
Less than 1	37
1–2	28
3–5	20
6–10	8
11–15	2
16–20	1
21+	1

REASON FOR LEAVING SERVICE	(%)
Resignation	
Other Business	28
Pay	1
Sick[b]	3
Did Not Report	6
Other[c]	8
Discharged/Dismissed	
Deserted	2
Disciplinary	8
Drunk	2
Other[d]	9
Other	
Better Location/Station	6
Promotion	3
Still Serving	9
Transfer	8

SOURCE: Register of Employees, U.S. Life-Saving Service, 1871(?)–1913(?), Records of the U.S. Coast Guard, RG26, National Archives, Washington, D.C.

NOTE: $N = 1{,}902$

[a] Totals do not add to 100 percent because of missing data.

[b] Sickness either of surfman or his family.

[c] Not recorded or entered simply as resigned.

[d] Usually recorded as discharged/dismissed, no reason given.

Despite low pay and no retirement system, the service managed to retain men to fill the ranks of surfmen. (Coast Guard Museum Northwest)

total of ninety-six surfmen who served at that station, compared with forty who served during the same time period at the isolated station at Cape Hatteras, North Carolina. As Kimball continually tried to explain to Congress, better pay would lure men away from the service, and the chances for being led away were naturally higher in the larger communities or urban areas. In isolated regions where there were fewer career options, men tended to stay in the service longer.

Promotions came slowly, and this may be another reason men left the service. In the Eleventh Life-Saving District only 3 percent of the surfmen serving during the years 1876 to 1913 were promoted to keeper. Eight percent were transferred; another six percent resigned to move to another station.

The statistics, and a few cryptic remarks in the personnel rolls, indicate that a surfman's life was not the well-ordered affair of myth. Twenty-one percent of the surfmen who served in the Eleventh Life-Saving

Like most lifesaving crews, this West Coast unit was composed of men middle-aged or older. The keeper (seated center with medal) is believed to be Albert Steam, who received the medal from the British government for his assistance to the English ship *Lammerlaw* in 1882. (Coast Guard Museum Northwest)

District were discharged or dismissed (see table 4). The reasons given were usually for such offenses as sleeping on watch or tampering with the patrol clock. Some surfmen were "disruptive" or could not get along with the keeper. One man was "saucy" to the keeper, and one surfman shot himself in the foot and tried to make it look accidental to avoid carrying out his duties. Another surfman was dismissed when he was caught taking a woman with him on beach patrol. A surfman stationed at St. Joseph, Michigan, was dismissed because he was afraid of the lifeboat capsizing drill that all crewmen had to be able to perform. Some men resigned because they found the U.S. Life-Saving Service "too confining." A few did not like the long periods of absence from their homes, stating they were "homesick." So what was the "average" surfman like who served on Lake Michigan during the period 1876 to 1913?

He was a United States citizen and residing in the state in which the

A boat crew underway (probably from Sandy Hook, New Jersey). (U.S. Coast Guard)

station was located. He was twenty-seven when he entered the service and had a background in fishing. He would serve no more than two years, and would probably leave after the first year possibly to seek better employment, especially if he was stationed in a larger community or urban area.

The men who served as keepers and surfmen in the U.S. Life-Saving Service were a more diverse group than the accepted myth. This group of rather ordinary men, some with very little formal education and from very humble means, accomplished a great deal. Robert F. Bennett notes that from 1878 to 1915, 28,121 vessels and 178,741 persons were involved

Lucian Clemons (left), first recipient (1876) of the Gold Life Saving Medal. (Institute for Great Lakes Research, Bowling Green State University)

Keeper W. W. Griesser, of Buffalo, N.Y. Thrown into the water from a lifeboat in November 1900, he grabbed a line, swam for nearly an hour to reach a man in distress, and pulled him to shore. He won the Gold Life Saving Medal for this heroic action. (National Archives)

with the services of the U.S. Life-Saving Service. Only 1,455 people lost their lives while exposed within the scope of U.S. Life-Saving operations.[14]

Perhaps a Joe Lincoln poem best captures the way that many people viewed the men of the U.S. Life-Saving Service:

He's a rigger, rower, swimmer, sailor, undertaker,
And he's good at every one of 'em the same,
And he risks his life for others in the quicksands and the breakers.
And a thousand wives and mothers bless his name.
He's an angel dressed in oilskins, he's a saint in a "sou'wester,"

Surfman Frederick T. Hatch, in the uniform of the U.S. Lighthouse Service, was one of only two men to win two Gold Life Saving Medals. (National Archives)

He's as plucky as they make, or ever can.
He's a hero born and bred, but it hasn't swelled his head,
And he's jest the U.S. Gov'ment's hired man.[15]

Behind the rather romantic facade of Lincoln's poem the fact remains that the men in the service faced a future with no retirement pay and very little disability compensation. They also faced the real possibility of being forced to resign when their physical examinations showed them to be incapable of withstanding the rigors of rescue work. What is amazing is that the keepers and surfmen nevertheless pushed out into gale-whipped seas, risking their lives and accomplishing so much for so little.

CHAPTER FIVE

Lifeboats and Surfboats

The technology of the nineteenth and early twentieth centuries determined the two basic methods the U.S. Life-Saving Service used in rescuing those stranded close to shore. The first and least complicated method was by small boat. This was also the most dangerous for the lifesavers. The second method was less dangerous, but more complicated, as it entailed establishing a strong line between the lifesavers on shore and those on the wrecked craft. (This method of rescue is discussed in chapter 6.) Small oar-powered boats were the only craft that could work close to shore when gale-whipped surf pounded the beach. A large sailing vessel stood an excellent chance of being driven ashore if it went to the assistance of a grounded ship. To understand the use of small boats in the service, it is necessary to know something about how the boats evolved and to understand how geography determined the type of boats used in the service.

The U.S. Life-Saving Service generally used two classes of small boats in rescues. Although any boat used to rescue someone in distress can be called a lifeboat, the service very clearly separated the boats into lifeboats and surfboats. A coastal lifeboat was more than twenty-seven feet long, was of stronger construction than a surfboat and with a deeper draft, and was self-bailing and self-righting. (Throughout this book, lifeboat, unless used in describing a boat launched from a ship, will mean coastal lifeboat; the U.S. Life-Saving Service and other rescue organizations dropped the "coastal" in describing their large rescue boats.) Unfortunately for the researcher, most newspaper reports of small boat rescues, and even some keepers' reports, use the term "lifeboat" instead of the more accurate "surfboat." The boats, however, were definitely not the same. Each was designed for a specific use and each reflected the geography of the different regions in which the U.S. Life-Saving Service operated.[1]

The lifeboats used in the United States are direct descendants of craft built in England. In 1785 Lionel Ludkin, a coach builder of Long Acre, London, was awarded a patent for an unsinkable boat. Ludkin had converted a Norway yawl, clinker built, double-ended, into a lifeboat by adding nine-inch-thick cork fenders along the gunwales, with cork beneath the thwarts and in spaces at the bow and stern, along with a heavy iron keel. Ludkin's design achieved the two most important characteristics in lifeboats: buoyancy and stability.[2]

Four years later, after a series of shipwrecks at the mouth of the Tyne River in northeast England, a group of citizens sponsored a contest to design a lifeboat. William Wouldhave, of South Shields, sent in the winning model. This is the earliest known documented plan for a self-righting boat and Wouldhave is credited with being the creator of the lifeboat. The model was a double-ender with a pronounced sheer, cork on the interior of the hull, a fairly straight keel, and airtight cases filled with cork at both ends. The judges of the contest, however, felt the boat needed further refinement and awarded Wouldhave only half the prize. Two of the judges then modified the design and asked Henry Greathead, a professional boatbuilder in South Shields, to build it. The changes were in the keel, to give it more buoyancy, and the boat closely resembled Ludkin's work.[3]

The boat, named the *Original,* was completed in 1790. It was a double-ender, clinker built. Thirty feet in length, it had a twenty-foot keel, a ten-foot beam, and a height at each end of five feet nine inches. The boat held plenty of cork, but it did not have airtight compartments; it was not self-righting and self-bailing; and it did not carry sails. All of this made the *Original,* in essence, a large surfboat with a good deal of buoyancy. Despite these shortcomings, it served as a lifeboat for forty years and saved hundreds of lives.[4]

In 1824 the National Institute for the Preservation of Life from Shipwreck, later to be called the Royal National Life Boat Institution, was

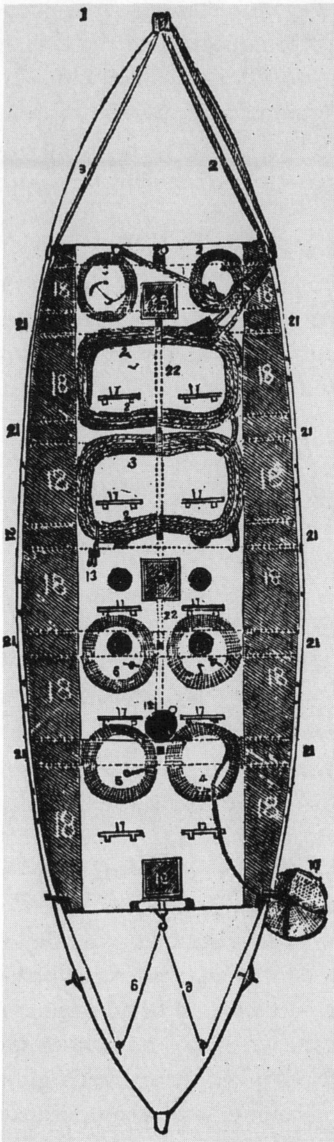

1. Anchor.
2. Cable.
3. Bow heaving-line or grapnel-rope and grapnel.
4. Drogue-rope.
5. Stern heaving-line.
6. } Veering-lines.
7. }
8. Jib outhaul or tack.
9. Mizzen-sheets.
10. Drogue.
11. Life-buoy.
12. Loaded cane, heaving-line, and tub.
13. Tailed block.
14. Pump-well hatch.
15. } Deck-ventilating hatches.
16. }
17. Foot-boards for rowers.
18. Side air-cases.
19. Relieving tubes and valves.
20. Samson's post.
21. Thwarts.
22. Central batten, to which the masts and boat-hooks are lashed.

DECK-PLAN OF SELF-RIGHTING LIFE-BOAT, SHOWING MANNER OF STOWING GEAR.

Plan of the service's earliest lifeboat. (*Regulations of the U.S. Life-Saving Service*, 1873) founded. The institute, quite naturally, began to study lifeboat designs. In 1826 Pellew Plenty, of Newbury, east of Bristol, built the first of at least a dozen boats. Plenty's design was also a double-ender with a large beam amidships. It contained a large amount of cork, plus air cases built along the inboard sides. As with previous boats, Plenty's craft had a high degree of buoyancy, but this lifeboat was also self-bailing through the use of six drain tubes.[5]

The next step in the development of the English lifeboat came in 1826 when George Palmer, of Essex, became deputy chairman of the National Lifeboat Institution. A member of Parliament, Palmer took a keen interest in lifeboat design and instituted the first practical attempt toward a partially self-righting lifeboat. The boat's self-bailing and self-righting features, however, were not reliable.[6]

The National Life Boat Institution was reorganized in 1851 and Algernon, Duke of Northumberland, also known as "the sailor duke," became its president. Later to become First Lord of the Admiralty, the duke took a strong interest in the institution and immediately upon taking office, he offered a one-hundred-guinea prize for the best model of an improved lifeboat. The duke pointed out that lifeboats then in use were very slow to bail, were not adequately self-righting, and were costly to build. The competition influenced the design of lifeboats for many years.[7] The committee appointed by the duke established a point system for judging the characteristics of the 250 entries submitted to it. The highest number of points, twenty, was given to "qualities as a rowing boat in all weathers," with "qualities as a sailing boat" receiving eighteen, "means of freeing boat of water rapidly" eight, and "power of self-righting" six. The maximum points a design could earn was one hundred.[8]

A boatbuilder from Great Yarmouth, James Beeching, won the contest with a total of eighty-four points. Beeching's boat was thirty-six feet in overall length, had a keel of thirty-one feet, a beam of nine feet nine inches, and a draft of three feet six inches. It was fitted with seven thwarts and pulled by twelve oars, double banked. It was self-righting, with raised air cases at both ends. Self-bailing was accomplished by twelve relief tubes through the bottom. The boat carried two and one-half tons of water ballast, was of lapstrake construction and furnished with an iron keel. It carried a lug foresail and mizzen, and Beeching claimed it would transport up to seventy survivors in addition to the lifeboat's crew. The estimated cost to build this boat was £250.[9] According to William D. Wilkinson, a leading authority on rescue boats, this "marks the first wholly successful self-righting lifeboat and established the quality of self-righting as a requisite in lifeboat design for the next 35 years."[10]

The Duke of Northumberland's committee felt that the Beeching boat could be improved upon. They directed one of their members, James Peake, assistant master shipwright of Her Majesty's Dockyard at Woolwich, to design a boat using the best components of many of the outstanding designs, including Beeching's.[11] Peake's boat was thirty feet in overall length, with an eight-foot-three-quarter-inch beam and a draft of three and one-half feet. It had cork as ballast for the whole length of the boat beneath the flooring and an iron keel. Air cases in the bow and stern were raised to increase overall buoyancy, and there was no water ballast. The boat could self-right in five seconds and completely self-bail through self-acting relief valves in the bottom in fifty-five seconds. The Peake boat was designed to carry thirty survivors in addition to its twelve-man crew. The boat was pulled by ten oars, double banked, and its sail rig was similar to that of the Beeching design.[12]

Peake's design was built at Woolwich at government expense. Instead of following Beeching's traditional lapstrake or clinker construction, Peake's plan called for the craft to incorporate double diagonal planking. Wilkinson notes that "all wooden hull lifeboats built for the institution since 1851 have used the Peake type of construction."[13] Successful trials of the Peake lifeboat were conducted at Brighton on 3 February 1852. With only minor modifications, three other boats were built and all were stationed on the Northumberland coast. The three boats and their carriages were financed by the Duke of Northumberland.[14] The remainder of 1852 saw additional trials by the institution and the beginning of a building program for a standard self-righting lifeboat for the organization. The standard boat that evolved combined all the best features of the Beeching and Peake designs and neither man, according to Wilkinson, can "be considered the sole inventor or developer."[15]

The lifeboat of the Royal National Life Boat Institution changed very little between 1853 and 1854, although several different sizes were built, ranging from eight to twelve oars, double banked, and thirty to thirty-four feet in length. More than one hundred boats of the thirty-foot type were built. Water ballast was reintroduced in a new design, and a centerboard was fitted to the institution's lifeboat in 1884. The basic hull design and construction, however, remained the same.[16] The story of the lifeboats of the U.S. Life-Saving Service begins with the standard lifeboat.

When Sumner I. Kimball began the reorganization of the U.S. Life-Saving Service in 1871, he also authorized a study of lifeboat and surfboat design in America and what improvements could be made. Capt. J. H. Merryman, USRM, superintendent of construction for the service, and later to become its chief inspector, was instrumental in the development of the U.S. Life-Saving Service's boats.

In June 1873 Secretary of the Treasury W. A. Richardson requested B. F. Stevens, the U.S. dispatch agent in London, to purchase the latest model of the self-bailing, self-righting lifeboat being used by the Royal National Life Boat Institution. The institution's officials informed Stevens that it was very difficult to launch one of the boats without a transportation and launching carriage, so a carriage was included in the transaction. The total cost for the boat, carriage, and other equipment from the builder, T. and W. Forrest and Son of Norway Yard, Limehouse, London, was £531.[17] The boat selected for the U.S. Life-Saving Service was thirty feet in overall length, seven feet one inch in beam, with a draft of three feet six inches. Hull construction was of double diagonal mahogany planking, with mahogany deck and iron keel. Large air chambers were at the bow and stern. A heavy iron keel provided the self-righting capability and four relieving valves, through the main deck, provided a self-bailing characteristic that was capable of freeing the boat of water in twenty-four seconds. There were four thwarts for eight oars, double banked, and the craft carried two standing lugs for sail.[18]

Self-bailing, self-righting lifeboat under sail. (U.S. Coast Guard)

Crewmen at the oars of lifeboat; young boy is in scaled-down keeper's uniform. (From the Jesse Besser Museum Collection, Alpena, Michigan)

The lifeboat and equipment arrived in New York City in early August 1873 and were placed aboard the U.S. Revenue cutter *Grant* for transport to Narragansett Bay, Rhode Island. Near the Narragansett Life-Saving Station, extensive trials were held under the direction of Captain Merryman and other officers. Merryman pointed out that there was "no doubt" that the lifesaving institutions of Europe were "far superior" in developing equipment to save those who shipwrecked on their coasts, but the coast of the United States brought special problems that would greatly hinder the use of the English lifeboat. The greatest difficulty was the weight of the boat and carriage.[19]

The English lifeboat was designed for a coast that is generally made up of rocky headlands or very steep sloping coastal areas. Heavy lifeboats could usually be launched by rampway or carriage directly into deep water or a sheltered harbor. If the boat had to be transported, it was usually for only a short distance and generally over good roads. Thus the weight of the boat was not a major factor. In the United States, however, the weight and size of a boat were legitimate concerns. In the first years of the service, most of the lifesaving stations were located on the eastern seaboard. In general, the stations were built along isolated stretches of sandy beaches and in areas of poor roads. Rescue by boat usually consisted of either launching a boat directly from the station over a short stretch of beach or pulling the craft on a carriage over a sandy beach and launching the boat into the surf. The boat most suited for this type of work was the surfboat, which was usually smaller than twenty-

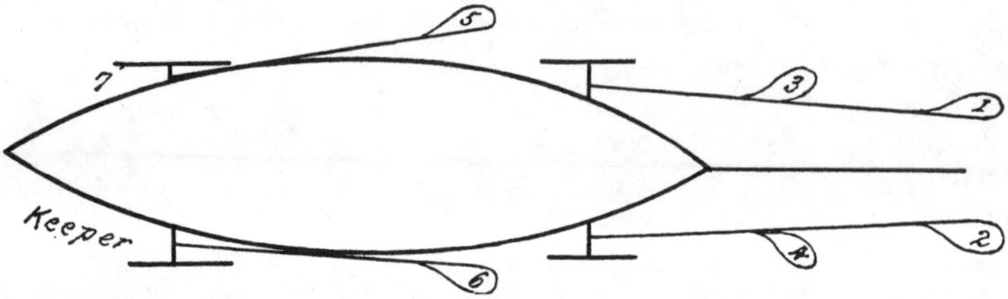

Surfboat and cart could be pulled to a site by the lifesavers. (*Regulations of the U.S. Life-Saving Service,* 1873)

six feet in length and weighed approximately seven hundred pounds. The size and weight of this type of craft made it ideal to transport over the sandy terrain, and the boats were easy to handle in a rough surf. In addition, the craft was used by surf fishermen, the former profession of many of the men who entered the U.S. Life-Saving Service. In the annual report of 1882 the service reported that the surfboat had been used 284 times, making 381 trips, while the lifeboat was used only 11 times, making 15 trips.[20]

The English lifeboat, however, was well suited for those locations where it could be launched from an inclined ramp into deep water and then rowed, or towed by a tug, to a wreck site. On the inland seas sailing ships were most likely to wreck at the narrow entrance to harbors when trying to reach shelter during a storm. Many of the stations along the Great Lakes were located within the shelter of a harbor. The heavy lifeboat could be quickly launched from an inclined ramp directly into the sheltered water of the harbor. The lifesavers then had only a short

Horses were sometimes used to haul lifesavers' equipment. (U.S. Coast Guard)

distance to row the heavy craft, and they had the advantage of a boat that could take the hardest punishment and still bring back its crew. Even so, the craft met with resistance from Great Lakes lifesavers. Like their fellow lifesavers on the eastern seaboard, the lakers felt the boat was too big and heavy. But, according to some reports, after crewmen saw what it could do in heavy weather, they came to regard it as "something almost supernatural," for it could withstand storms "when the most powerful tugs and steamcraft refused to go out of the harbor."[21] The lifeboat served primarily on the Great Lakes and the West Coast, where it could be launched from an inclined ramp.

Captain Merryman set about designing a smaller version of the English lifeboat that would be better suited for use in this country. Merryman designed two new types of lifeboat. One was of galvanized iron construction, the other of wood. The iron boat did not make it into service, but the wooden boat did.[22] Merryman's design called for a self-bailing, self-righting boat of twenty-six feet eight inches in length, with a beam of seven feet three and a quarter inches and a draft of one foot nine inches. Construction included double diagonal planking gunwale to gunwale of three-eighths-inch mahogany with copper fastenings, an iron keel, four thwarts, and six copper relieving tubes with self-acting valves mounted vertically through the hull from the main deck. Weight without the crew and equipment was about forty-two hundred pounds, and with the crew and equipment the boat weighed about seven thousand pounds. The craft had air cases at both ends and five air cases of canvas-covered wood mounted fore and aft on each side of the main deck under side battens. The hold between the end air cases and under the main deck was divided into three watertight compartments that were filled with fourteen ballast cases of cork. The lifeboat was pulled by eight oars, double banked, and carried a two-mast standing lug rig with jib. The boat was modified very little over its years of service.[23]

The first Merryman boats were completed in 1876 by two New York City boatbuilders: Stephen Roberts, of Harlem, and D. Blackburn. Eventually, other New York boatbuilders began to construct the craft. In 1893 Frederick C. Beebe, of Greenport, Long Island, built seven of the lifeboats. Beebe was to become the largest single contractor to the service. Other firms in the Great Lakes and one on the West Coast received contracts to build the craft. At least seventy-seven of the boats were built. More than two-thirds were constructed in New York City, and more than 80 percent went to stations on the Great Lakes.[24] Captain Merryman's office was in New York City, and he was able to closely supervise the work. In addition, at the time New York City had more boatbuilders capable of building the lifeboat.[25]

In the late 1870s and 1880s an effort was made by some officials of the U.S. Life-Saving Service, including Capt. David P. Dobbins, superintendent of the Ninth U.S. Life-Saving Service District, at Buffalo, New York, to combine the best features of the surfboat with those of the Merryman lifeboat. "Experience soon showed this approach to be impractical" and the design was dropped.[26] The U.S. Life-Saving Service began to build a larger version of the Merryman boat in 1891. This new boat was thirty-four feet in length and essentially the same as the smaller boat in construction and other features. It had a sprit rig and a centerboard, along with water ballast, and was pulled by ten oars, double banked.[27]

The U.S. Life-Saving Service lifeboat was used in an unusual rescue by a station on Lake Superior. On 17 November 1887 "one of the worse [*sic*] northeasters that ever swept over Lake Superior" passed over the lake.[28] Within forty-eight hours more than thirty ships were wrecked, with the loss of nearly forty lives.[29] On 18 November some townspeople of Marquette, Michigan, ventured out onto the city's breakwater to view the storm-tossed lake. Through the still blowing snow, the onlookers could dimly see shapes to the east that appeared to be ships. What the crowd had spied was the "large steam barge" *Robert Wallace,* with a crew of fifteen, and her consort, the *David Wallace,* with nine sailors aboard. Both were bound from Duluth to Buffalo with a cargo of wheat. Because of the distance involved and the blowing snow, it was impossible to tell whether the ships were in distress, so a small group loaded a yawl onto a cart and set out to see if the two vessels needed assistance. The search party found that the two ships had grounded by the stern, some four hundred yards offshore. The wind-whipped waves broke completely over both ships. Nevertheless, the dauntless group of rescuers launched their small yawl into the surf in an attempt to reach the wrecks. The boat was driven back before it even reached halfway. A tug arrived shortly afterward and tried to reach the vessels, but to no avail.[30]

By one o'clock in the afternoon a large crowd of onlookers had gathered on the beach opposite the grounded ships. Someone thought to dispatch a driver and a team of horses to a nearby mill for an old mortar stored there, thinking it might be used to shoot a line to the sailors on the wrecks. Meanwhile another unsuccessful attempt was made to reach the ships by small boat. Through the driving snow the onlookers could see the sailors aboard the vessels trying to float lines to the beach with water butts, but the undertow and waves swept the lines away.[31]

By now darkness was fast approaching and the only hope left seemed to be the old mortar. The ordnance piece, however, was spiked and a good deal of time was consumed in finding a shop to drill it out. Not until six o'clock in the evening was the mortar finally set up on the beach. A measure of gunpowder was placed in the piece and a line attached to a projectile. The mortar was fired, but the projectile fell far short of the wrecks. The line was retrieved and a larger charge placed in the ordnance piece. This time the mortar blew up. Fortunately, no one was injured.[32]

All means of rescue had been exhausted by the well-intentioned crowd. Hope was lost. Twenty-four sailors were about to lose their lives within sight of a large group of helpless onlookers. The captain of the tug *Gillette,* however, felt that as a last resort the U.S. Life-Saving Station at Ship Canal, Michigan, should be notified, although it was located 110 miles from the wrecks. A message was hastily dispatched.

The telegram was delivered to Keeper Albert Ocha by a circuitous route. It was transmitted from Marquette to Houghton, some six miles from the lifesaving station, then taken by the tug *James W. Croze* the remaining distance. Keeper Ocha and his crew, not knowing how difficult the rescue might be, placed the beach apparatus (the equipment needed to shoot a projectile and line to a wreck) and the lifeboat aboard the tug and proceeded to Houghton. The railroad had promised a special train to transport the lifesavers and their equipment to Marquette. As soon as the tug tied up at Houghton, the lifesavers, assisted by volunteers, quickly loaded their equipment aboard a flat car. Ocha and his crew climbed into a passenger car and the train set out on a 110-mile dash through the snowy night.[33]

Despite the heavy snow en route the entire journey took only about four hours. The train paused briefly on its way so Keeper Ocha could send a message to Marquette to have lanterns and teams of horses to transport the lifesavers and their equipment waiting on their arrival. Shortly before midnight the train pulled into the station at Marquette and willing volunteers helped the lifesavers transport their equipment to the site of the wrecks. On 19 November at about one o'clock in the morning the lifesavers arrived on the beach opposite the two ships. Checking his equipment, Keeper Ocha found that the lifeboat's rudder had been damaged. He decided to try the line-throwing equipment. The line fell over the stern of one of the ships, but the seas were washing so heavily over the vessels that the sailors, who were huddled in the bow section, could not safely move to the stern. Keeper Ocha knew the only hope was to launch the lifeboat, no matter what its condition.[34]

At two o'clock in the morning, the crew rammed the boat into the breaking seas. Two sand bars were crossed, with very high surf at each crossing. Passing over the first bar, the lifeboat shipped three seas of freezing water, bending the irons of the rudder and splitting its wood. Keeper Ocha was forced to put back to shore for hasty repairs. While his men were working on the rudder, Ocha again tried the line-throwing equipment, but to no avail. If the sailors aboard the two ships were to be saved it would have to be by the lifeboat.[35]

The boat was again launched and the lifesavers pulled hard and "desperately" over the two sand bars, again shipping several seas.[36] The high freezing winds caused the spray and water to form a sheen of ice on both the boat and the lifesavers. Keeper Ocha gradually worked his boat close to the ice-shrouded *Robert Wallace*. Because of the ice on the lifeboat and the high winds and seas, only nine of the ship's crew of fifteen could be taken on this first trip to the beach. Once these men were safely on the beach, the lifeboat was relaunched and the remainder of the *Robert Wallace*'s crew were safely put ashore. For the fourth time the weary lifesavers shoved their craft into the pounding surf of Lake Superior to rescue the nine sailors aboard the *David Wallace*. Keeper Ocha and his crew had been at their oars for more than six hours, and each passage across the storm-tossed lake coated the men with ice. The constant shipping of water and the coating of ice caused the "buoyant boat to [be filled] to the gunnels."[37] The U.S. Life-Saving Service's official report graphically describes the fourth rescue trip: "Again and again the boat was flooded, and driven astern; on the second reef she was nearly thrown end over

Surfmen straining at the oars and keeper at the sweep oar symbolize the U.S. Life-Saving Service. (Weckler Collection, Michigan Maritime Museum, South Haven, Michigan)

end; the rudder split so much and got so weak that she had to be managed almost solely by the oars, involving double skill and labor; and her valiant crew were incessantly drenched with the icy water, which froze upon their clothing as fast as it struck, and thickened the bitter mail in which they were sheathed."[38] It took Keeper Ocha approximately one hour to reach and maneuver his boat alongside the *David Wallace*. The nine sailors tumbled into the lifeboat and the lifesavers made their last journey to the beach. As soon as the lifeboat reached the shore, the people on the beach rushed to the boat, guided the sailors and lifesavers to roaring fires they had kept on the beach, and served them hot coffee. By 20 November Keeper Ocha and his crew were back at the Ship Canal Station.[39]

The rescue of the crews from the *Robert Wallace* and the *David Wallace* was a journalistic delight. Reporters made much of the long dash through the snowy night by train, followed by the four difficult boat passages through storm-tossed seas. Indeed, it had all the ingredients of a dime novel. But this was real-life adventure. The rescue is an excellent example of just how rugged the lifeboat could be: although filled to the gunwales and coated with ice, the buoyancy of the craft allowed it to remain afloat. The resilient lifeboat and its indomitable crew prevented Lake Superior from claiming the lives of twenty-four sailors.

In 1899 the U.S. Life-Saving Service selected a thirty-four foot Merryman lifeboat to evaluate the results of installing a twelve-horsepower gasoline engine within it. Successful tests of the boat were conducted at the station located at Marquette, Michigan, by Keeper Henry Cleary. The installation of the engine and related equipment added approximately fifteen hundred pounds to the lifeboat.[40] By 1906 the service was using a twenty-five-horsepower standard engine, which weighed less than one-half of the first experimental engine. The 1906 version was installed in the after air case and drove an eighteen-inch three-bladed propeller at nine hundred revolutions per minute. A seventy-five-gallon gas tank was installed in the forward air case, with a twenty-five-gallon auxiliary tank located in the same space. If the boat capsized, the motor was stopped by a circuit breaker that cut off the engine's ignition circuit.[41] In 1906 Capt. C. H. McClellan, inspector and superintendent of construction for the service, noted that even though the addition of gasoline engines to the thirty-four foot lifeboats made "a pronounced improvement and added greatly to the efficiency of the boat," one problem continued: the engine caused a "loss in carrying capacity, because of the great weight of the motor."[42] Thirty-three years after the lifeboat was introduced into the U.S. Life-Saving Service, officers were still commenting on its

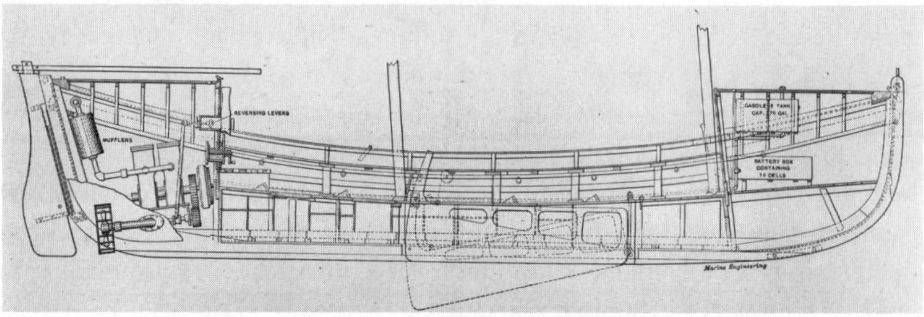

Longitudinal section of the thirty-four-foot motorized lifeboat (1900). (Mariner's Museum, Newport News, Virginia)

weight. Nevertheless, the successful introduction of the gasoline engine as a power source for the lifeboat marked the last stage of development of these boats in the U.S. Life-Saving Service. The use of powerful motorized lifeboats was just beginning; the primary employment of these boats would be during the U.S. Coast Guard era.

The boat most used by the U.S. Life-Saving Service was the surfboat. Surfboats are generally light, open shallow draft craft, usually between twenty and twenty-seven feet in length and able to be launched directly from the beach into the surf.[43] The boat was popular with surf fishermen

Crews often named their lifeboats; 1910 crew of Neah Bay, Washington, dubbed one of their motorized boats *Audacious.* (Coast Guard Museum Northwest)

of the eastern seaboard, who made up a large portion of the U.S. Life-Saving Service's crews on that coast. The lightness of the craft made the boat easy for small crews to handle, and the boat was easily maneuverable and performed well in short pulls in heavy surf.

In the early years of the service there was no standardized surfboat. The boat builders of each coastal region of the eastern seaboard were watermen who provided modifications to their craft to meet the needs of their local area. In 1872 Capt. Robert B. Forbes, of the Massachusetts Humane Society, wrote that he could not recommend any one type of boat that would be successful in New Jersey, Long Island, Nantucket, Cape Cod, and other locations. Captain Forbes felt that watermen in these areas had their "own ideas" as to the type of craft "they require when they are to risk their lives to save life and property." For example, the surfmen on the New Jersey coast preferred a boat that had a "flat bottom, broad stern, sloping sides and considerable sheer, built of cedar or light corrugated iron." Further to the north, on Nantucket Island, Massachusetts, surfmen preferred "light wooden clincher-built boats, with a large beam and considerable sheer, pulling long oars, single bank, and steering like whale boats"; whereas their nearby neighbors along Cape Cod used "full built, flat round bottomed cedar built boats, both ends alike."[44] A large variety of surfboats were used throughout the entire history of the service. It is beyond the scope of this chapter to detail all the surfboats used by the service. The New Jersey type will serve as a representative.

The New Jersey surfboat can trace its origins to the early Swedish settlers of south Jersey.[45] The first documented information on the use of surfboats comes from an 1846 report to the state legislature. The report, which concerned charges leveled against the coastal residents of Monmouth County for refusing to help those in distress, robbing the dead, and other incidents arising from the wreck of the *John Minburn,* made reference to a "surf-boat." (The charges, incidentally, were not proved.) The surfboats, crewed by four oarsmen and a coxswain, were transported to the beach on a wagon drawn by a team of horses. In 1846 there were ten surfboats along the Jersey shore.[46] The surfboat developed for lifesaving work was the "same as the smaller beach skiffs, developed for fishing."[47] The skiffs were built to meet the particular features of the state's coastline. That is, when strong winds drove the seas over relatively shallow water and sand bars, short, steep seas were generated. Fishermen needed a boat that was light enough to be handled by a small crew and could be launched and landed through heavy surf.

San Francisco lifesavers drill with their lifeboat. (San Francisco Maritime National Historical Park)

The first recorded skiffs were approximately fifteen feet in length, with a five-foot beam. They had round bilges, sloping transoms, a slightly rockered plank heel, and a strong sheer. The boat was lapstrake, with white cedar over sawn frames. Fastenings were of copper rivets or clinch nails. Planks were in short lengths to make a flexible, watertight hull. The U-shaped transom was raked approximately thirty degrees. "The wide-bottom plank with tapered ends provided a resting surface when beached, while its rocker made turning easy." The skiffs were rowed or sailed with a sprit rig and jib.[48]

Congressman William Newell's 1848 report, which led to federal funding for lifesaving stations and equipment, mentioned that the lifeboats aboard ships were unable to withstand the surf on New Jersey's coastal bars. The only craft suitable for this was the surfboat, indicating that the boat was already well established on the state's beaches. However, there was no detailed description of the boat.[49]

In 1858 the secretary of the treasury reported on a series of tests conducted on surfboats at Sea Bright, New Jersey. Two of the boats tested, reportedly of an old New Jersey design, were described as being constructed of cedar, clinker built, with a square stern, and pulled by six oars. The boats were twenty-six feet in length, with a twenty-two-foot keel and seven-foot beam; they weighed about 950 pounds.[50]

Another boat, a Bunker's model, was built of three-quarter-inch cedar, clinker type, fastened with copper and riveted, with a square stern. This model was pulled by four oars and had detached air chambers at the stern, stem, and under the thwarts at each side. The craft was twenty-four feet, eight inches in length, weighed around seven hundred pounds, and was described "as possessing great buoyancy, lightness, and strength."[51]

The U.S. Life-Saving Service used a variety of surfboats along the eastern seaboard because boat builders usually added their own special refinements based on conditions in their local area. The boats were named for the areas where the builders resided. Stations had Long Branch, Squan, and Mayville models, along with others, in their boathouses. The most common were the Long Branch and Squan. According to Peter J. Guthorn, no "two boats, by the same builder, were quite the same size, regardless of model." But the boats fell into three general sizes: twenty-three, twenty-five, and twenty-seven feet.[52]

The New Jersey type of surfboat was well suited for lifesaving, for it took into account the topography of the eastern seaboard. The craft's lightness made its easy to launch from the beach directly into the surf and easy to transport over sandy beaches. The generous sheer of the boat and its lightness made it a very maneuverable boat in the surf. As the boat returned to the beach through the breakers, the action of the waves

Surfboat about to be launched from its cart. (San Francisco Maritime National Historical Park)

on the raked surface of the stern served to lift it and allow the waves to pass beneath.[53]

Surfboats were usually used for distances of a few hundred yards offshore. On 22 December 1885, however, the crew of the station at Cape Hatteras, in North Carolina, performed a rescue that the service was to

Crew of Salisbury Beach, Massachusetts, prepares to launch surfboat during drill. (U.S. Coast Guard)

Lifesavers of Nome, Alaska, Station prepare to beach their boat. (Coast Guard Museum Northwest)

record as "one of the most heroic feats in the annals of the Life-Saving Service." They rowed five miles out to sea to rescue nine sailors from the barkentine *Ephraim Williams.*[54]

On 18 December 1885 the *Ephraim Williams,* of Providence, Rhode Island, was bound from Savannah, Georgia, with a cargo of lumber when it struck a severe storm near Frying Pan Shoals. The intensity of the gale caused the ship to become waterlogged and out of control. For three days the *Ephraim Williams* drifted helplessly southward, wallowing among seas that were described as "running mountains high." The barkentine began to drift dangerously close to the shoals on 21 December, and the skipper ordered her anchor dropped in an effort to keep from drifting into the shallows. The storm was so strong that the hook would not hold and the *Ephraim Williams* began to drag. Crews at Durant's, Creed's Hill, Cape Hatteras, and Big Kinnakeet stations had all spotted the hapless barkentine and followed her as she drifted out of control. Eventually, all the lifesaving crews had gathered at the Cape Hatteras Station, but "such a fearful surf was thundering in" and the ship lay so far off shore that "it was absolutely impossible for them to do anything." The lifesavers remained at the Cape Hatteras Station awaiting daylight to find out if the *Ephraim Williams* would clear the shoals. Dawn's light revealed that the barkentine had missed the shoals and "fetched up" in surf that, in the judgment of old-time Cape Hatteras surfmen, was the "heaviest and most dangerous they had seen for years." The ship was stranded six or seven miles northeast of the Cape Hatteras Station and about five miles offshore from the Big Kinnakeet Station.

Most of the Big Kinnakeet crew was at the Cape Hatteras Station; they set out for their own unit to ready their boat. Exhausted from the long night's vigil and the rush back to their station, the crew ate a quick breakfast to restore their strength. While they were finishing, Keeper Benjamin B. Dailey, of the Cape Hatteras Station, arrived with his crew and the station's surfboat drawn on a carriage by horses. Keeper Patrick H. Etheridge, of the Creed's Hill Station, was among this group, substituting for an absent member of Dailey's crew. It was now approximately ten o'clock on the morning of 22 December, and the lifesavers had no indication that anyone was alive aboard the *Ephraim Williams*. Then they spotted a distress flag flying from the ship. Both lifesaving crews began to make preparations for the seemingly impossible pull of at least five miles in mountainous seas.

The two crews lashed down everything that might break loose in the boat, and despite the piercing wind they stripped off any clothing that might impede them in the event of a capsize. The men then donned their cork lifejackets and shoved their boats into the waters of the inner bar. Keeper Dailey and his lifesavers were the first to shove off into an "almost unbroken wall of tumultuous water."

Keeper Dailey's boat managed to get over the breakers of the inner bar, which were "immense in themselves"; then the surfboat's crew faced the full fury of the sea at the outer bar a half mile farther out. Witnesses on the shore felt that for any boat to withstand the pounding seas was a "forlorn hope." But Dailey held his boat in check while he waited for a slach, a brief period when the seas slacken. After a short period the slach arrived and Dailey gave the order for his crew to give way together. The boat shot past the bar. The Big Kinnakeet Station's surfboat and crew, with Keeper Scarborough in charge, arrived at the outer bar a few minutes later. They also waited for a slach, but none appeared. "Very much against their inclination," Scarborough's crew were forced to turn back.

Meanwhile, Keeper Dailey's crew continued to fight the seas in their long pull to the *Ephraim Williams*. The waves were so steep that witnesses on the beach could at times see the entire interior of the boat, and there was a real danger of the surfboat's pitch-poling, that is, being flipped end-over-end. The lifesavers rowed for approximately two hours to reach the stranded ship. The effort and endurance required of the seven men to pull the five miles is difficult to imagine.

Once near the *Ephraim Williams* Keeper Dailey faced the task of getting the nine sailors from the ship into the plunging surfboat. The high seas made it impossible to lay the boat alongside the barkentine, so Dailey dropped the boat's anchor off the *Ephraim Williams*'s quarter. He then instructed the captain of the ship to pass a line to the surfboat. With the anchor line played slowly out from the small boat and the boat pulled by the line from the ship, Dailey was able to place the surfboat close enough to take the sailors aboard one at a time. As soon as the *Ephraim Williams*'s crew were in the surfboat, Dailey weighed anchor and started for shore. The boat, with sixteen men aboard, was so heavily laden that it was down almost to her gunwales. On the run to the beach, Keeper Etheridge relieved Dailey at the sweep oar, so that Dailey could rig and tend a sea drogue to steady the deeply laden boat. The return, with the high following seas, went faster than the outbound struggle, and lifesavers and rescued sailors were soon being helped out of the boat onto the shore.

The U.S. Life-Saving Service called the efforts of Keeper Benjamin B. Dailey and his crew "one of the most daring rescues by the Life-Saving Service since its organization" and awarded the entire boat crew the Gold Life Saving Medal. The U.S. Revenue Cutter Service officer who investigated the wreck and rescue commented:

> I do not believe that a greater act of heroism is recorded than that of Dailey and his crew on this momentous occasion. These poor, plain men, dwellers upon the lonely sands of Hatteras, took their lives in their hands, and, at the most imminent risk, crossed the most tumultuous sea that any boat within the memory of living men had ever attempted on that bleak coast, and all for what? That others might live to see home and friends. The thought of reward or mercenary appeal never once entered their minds. Duty, their sense of obligation, and the credit of the Service impelled them on to do their mighty best.

By 1880 some of the U.S. Life-Saving Service's surfboats became self-righting and self-bailing. The Beebe-McLellan surfboat was double-ended and of lapstrake construction. The boat, however, was almost twice as heavy as the twenty-five-foot New Jersey boat and was not as popular among some old-time surfmen.[55] In 1912 Noel T. Methley noted that the Beebe-McLellan surfboat was now the craft most favored on the eastern seaboard. The boat by this time was twenty-five to twenty-seven feet in length, with an average size of twenty-five feet. It had a beam of seven feet and carried from twelve to fifteen people in addition to her

A 1909 rescue near San Francisco. (San Francisco Maritime National Historical Park)

crew of seven. The craft was built of cedar with white oak frames, had end air cases, and side cases beneath the thwarts. The boat was not self-righting, but was "insubmersible." The crew was trained in righting the boat themselves in case of capsizing. The boats were self-bailing and could be rigged with one mast, and jib, and sprit rig. Steering was accomplished with a sweep oar, and the boat weighed approximately one thousand pounds. By 1912 some of the surfboats were fitted with an eight-horsepower gasoline engine.[56]

The design of small boats used by the U.S. Life-Saving Service blended the technology of the times and a knowledge of the geography of the service's operating area. Although useful for work in extremely rough weather, lifeboats were suited for only certain areas of U.S. Life-Saving Service operations. The best locations were on the Great Lakes and along the West Coast, where the boat could be launched down an inclined ramp into deep water. (Not until 1899, when the service first experimented with gasoline-powered lifeboats, was the craft used more often and at more stations. If the service had continued after 1915 the gasoline-powered boats might have been placed at other locations, thus improving the range of stations' operations.)

The surfboat was light and could be easily transported over the sandy beaches of the eastern seaboard, and most lifesavers were familiar with it. In 1891 the lifeboat was used 81 times, whereas the surfboat was employed in more than 492 instances. Similar usage figures are given throughout the history of the service.[57] Even where lifeboats were located, most units also had a surfboat: the lifeboat for extremely rough weather, the surfboat for other rescues.[58] The small oar-powered (and later gasoline-powered) boats used by the U.S. Life-Saving Service were technology's answer to rescuing those shipwrecked close to the beach in the nineteenth and early twentieth century. The annals of the U.S. Life-Saving Service are filled with accounts of thousands of daring rescues in these small boats, which offered shipwrecked sailors the best rescue craft of the time and the best chance to survive the dangers of shipwreck.

CHAPTER SIX

Smoke and Shot

Since time out of mind shoreside rescuers have struggled with the frustrating question, How do you help people stranded close to the beach? One obvious means of helping a distressed ship close to shore is to pass a strong line to the sailors. But how do you get a line to a ship across storm-tossed waves? Spears, arrows, crossbows, even kites were used, with varying degrees of success, in attempts to pass a line to a grounded ship.

The advent of sturdy lifeboats did not solve the problem, for no boat—no matter how well designed—can easily withstand the awesome power of high surf in shallow water. In the mid-1700s Ergott Schaefer, a weaver in Kolberg, Prussia, wrote to Frederick the Great that he believed a mortar could be devised to carry a line from shore to a wrecked ship. Frederick sent the letter to the inspector general of artillery, who declared the idea impractical. Two decades later, Capt. George Manby, a British Merchant Marine officer, developed just such a mortar and it became an essential weapon in the lifesaver's war against the sea.[1]

On 29 December 1807 Henry Trengrouse, a cabinetmaker from Heston, Cornwall, watched the surf beat the frigate *Anson* to pieces on the rocks near Land's End. Trengrouse, along with a horror-struck crowd, watched powerless as the crew of one hundred men perished within a few hundred yards of safety. This disaster caused Trengrouse to seek a lightweight means of propelling a line to a ship. His answer was the rocket.

Trengrouse spent a decade in perfecting a line-carrying rocket. On 28 April 1818 he conducted a demonstration for the army of two types of line-carrying rockets. One, an eight-ounce model with a mackerel line attached, reached a range of 180 yards; the other, a one-pound device, propelled the line some 212 yards.[2]

In Europe the rocket became one of the mainstays in establishing a line between ship and shore. The U.S. Life-Saving Service and its predecessors, however, preferred to use the mortar and later the Lyle gun, which was a cannonlike device. Robert F. Bennett notes that although New Jersey congressman William Newell's legislation provided for rockets, the language of the bill establishing the federal presence in lifesaving indicated that they were to be used for signaling, "not as actual conveyances to establish communications between ship and shore."[3]

The Massachusetts Humane Society took its cues for rescue equipment from the Royal National Life Boat Institution. By 1845 the society's eighteen stations were equipped with mortars. Capt. Robert B. Forbes, president of the society, formed committees to evaluate and keep abreast of the lifesaving technology of Europe. Thus in 1848 when the federal government came into the picture, mortars were well established as a means of passing a line from the beach to a stranded craft. This enabled the federal government to enjoy the benefit of proven and tested equipment. Newell's ten-thousand-dollar appropriation helped to pay for further testing and development of the equipment.[4]

In the winter of 1848–49, Capt. Douglas Ottinger, of the U.S. Revenue Marine Service, began to test the equipment for use along the New Jersey coast. Ottinger ruled out the use of carronades, as their muzzle velocity parted the shotlines. The captain next turned to rockets. He conducted the tests at Sandy Hook, New Jersey, and to simulate a wrecked ship, the U.S. Revenue Marine's cutter *Pleasonton* anchored some 250 yards to seaward. Ottinger also experimented with the improved Manby mortar. This mortar was made of brass, had a five-and-a-half-inch bore, and was designed to use an extra-heavy charge of black powder. It could throw a line attached to a ball-like projectile 310 yards. The problem with the mortar—which became known as an eprouvette mortar—was twofold. First, the range was too short. Wrecks along the coast of England usually occurred within 150 yards of the beach, but ships wrecked along New Jersey's seacoast often grounded up to twice that distance away.

Maj. David A. Lyle, U.S. Army, perfected the line-throwing gun and apparatus used to establish a line between the beach and a wreck. (U.S. Coast Guard)

The only way to increase the range was through a larger charge, which led to the second problem. With a larger charge of black powder, the shotline would part. A series of experiments by Ottinger led to the attachment of a spiral wire to the projectile and the shotline. With the right amount of powder and the spiral wire, the mortar fired a twenty-four-pound projectile 421 yards. But Ottinger felt the mortar could not be expected to perform consistently beyond 320 yards.

Ottinger chose to solve the problem of what type of device to use by placing both rockets and eprouvette mortars at the first stations, and these devices remained in the federal service until 1871, when they were replaced by the cast-iron Parrott gun. In 1878 the Parrott gun was replaced by a gun designed by Lt. David A. Lyle, of the U.S. Army. The Lyle gun became the standard device employed for line throwing by the U.S. Life-Saving Service and was used until the 1960s.[5]

In 1875 the secretary of the treasury requested assistance from the secretary of war in developing improvements to the line-throwing apparatus. The U.S. Ordnance Board and Capt. James H. Merryman, of the U.S. Revenue Marine Service, were detailed to work on the project. By 1877 the work had bogged down because of the board's other duties, and Merryman appealed to the board to assign a special officer to the project. Lyle received the call.[6]

After two years of testing all the line-throwing devices in use, Lyle began to experiment with his own modifications to existing equipment. He received permission from the municipal authorities of Springfield, Massachusetts, and a private owner, to establish a test firing range. The range ran 687 yards and passed through part of the municipality of Springfield.[7] Before each shot Lyle had to post guards to stop traffic on a road that passed through the range. The site "enabled many idlers, especially boys, to congregate in the vicinity of the plane of fire," complained Lyle. "The delays and annoyances due to these causes were many and often times very troublesome. All appurtenances of the range had to be set up and removed at each visit to prevent their wanton destruction by tramps and thoughtless boys." The distractions prompted Lyle, in 1878, to transfer the experiments to a beach at Sandy Hook, New Jersey.

The gun Lyle developed looks like a short cannon. It is made of brass and weighs 163 pounds. For a carriage, Lyle chose iron-bound oak. For elevation settings, there is a notched wooden block. The projectile is best described as a "sash-weight-with-eyebolt." The eyebolt remains outside the cannon and, when fired, pulls the light shotline. Although longer ranges could be obtained with the gun, Lyle felt a hawser beyond six hundred yards could not be tightened enough to keep it above the surf, and he thought accuracy was more important than extreme long range.

Lyle made no claims of originality, noting that his work evolved directly from Manby's mortar. He spent the rest of his career with the Ordnance Department and remained a member of the Board of Lifesaving Devices under the Treasury Department. He died at St. Davis, Pennsylvania, on 10 October 1937, at the age of 92.[8]

Once a means of propelling a line to a stranded ship was developed, the U.S. Life-Saving Service used hundreds of yards of lines, blocks, and other paraphernalia to get a heavy hawser out to a ship. The first line shot over by the Lyle gun was the shotline. Made of hemp, unbleached linen, or nylon, the line ranged from 4/32 of an inch in diameter (number four line) to 9/32 of an inch (number nine line) and from 1,830 to 2,100 feet in length. Number seven and nine lines were most commonly used because the lighter lines tended to break. When wet, all lines tended to part, especially in a strong wind.[9]

The shotline was stored in a wooden faking box. Within the box was a framework containing a series of wooden pegs around which the line was faked (coiled). Before the line was faked, a false bottom with holes bored to fit over the pegs was inserted. The line was then faked on the pegs, each alternating tier being faked in the opposite direction of the

Equipment used for rescue by breeches buoy or lifecar: sand anchor is in front of shovels, along with heavy hawser; to right of shovels are Lyle gun, shotline, and projectile; breeches buoy, in front of shotline, sits on top of wooden crotch used to raise the hawser above the surf. (U.S. Coast Guard)

one before. To prepare the shotline for firing, the faking box was turned bottom side up and the false bottom carefully pushed out. The line now rested on the cover, which was inclined forty-five degrees in the direction of the firing. The faking of the line required a certain degree of skill. If improperly faked, the shotline would snarl and break as the projectile pulled it out of the box.

Once the shotline reached the distressed ship, the lifesavers on the beach would bend the shotline to a bight (loop) of a piece of one-and-a-half-inch-circumference line. The length of the doubled line, as measured from the two "bitter ends" to the bight, was at least equal to the distance

Surfmen fake (coil) a shotline over pegs in a faking box. (U.S. Coast Guard)

Pegs were removed from faking box, then box was aimed toward wreck. Shotline was tied to projectile. (U.S. Coast Guard)

from shore to the wreck. A half length of this line, known as the "whip," was roved through a single-sheave block so as to place the block near the bight. Attached to the top of the block itself was a piece of line several feet long, called a "tail." The shotline was made fast to the one-and-a-half-inch line and fastened to both parts of the bight a few feet above the block, securing the block and tail within the bight. Attached near the block was a tablet, called a "tally board," containing instructions, in French and English, on how to rig the whip.

Once the shotline reached the crew of a grounded ship, they could haul out the attached bight, the secured block and tail, and the tally board. The instructions on the board told the sailors to remove the shotline and tally board and to secure the tail of the block to an upright spar. The lifesavers then had a means of hauling additional objects to the ship, which were joined to the bitter ends of the whip. Once both bitter ends of the whip were joined, or an object attached to the ends, the rig resembled a horizontal clothesline used in some apartments.

Next, a heavy four-inch hawser was attached to the whip. The hawser also had a tally board attached, which directed the sailors to make the rope fast about eighteen inches above where the whip was tied off. This last phase of the work ensured a strong connection between ship and shore.

The next step on the part of the lifesavers was to raise the hawser high enough to clear the sea. The hawser was placed in an X-shaped crotch made of two two-by-three-inch pieces of hardwood about ten feet long and bolted together near the top. Near the end of the shore side of the hawser, a deep hole was dug to bury the "sand anchor," two pieces of crossed hardwood, six feet long, eight inches wide, and two inches thick, and bolted together at their center. Attached to the center of the sand anchor was an iron ring. The sand anchor was buried in the sand, with only the iron ring above the surface of the beach. A block and tackle, with a hook attached, was placed in the iron ring and the other end was used to take up the slack in the hawser. Raising the hawser with the crotch and tightening with the block and tackle ensured that the hawser would remain above the surf.

With a strong rope bridge to the ship, the lifesavers could now use one of two systems to bring the sailors to safety. One method entailed using a breeches buoy, a device like a large life buoy with canvas trousers attached. A small block and single sheave had four lines attached to the life ring. The block and sheave of the breeches buoy was then placed on the hawser and the whip was attached to the block of the breeches buoy. The lifesavers then pulled on the whip and the breeches buoy traveled along the hawser to the ship. The shipwrecked sailor stepped into the life buoy, signaled the shore that he was ready, and was pulled to safety. The other method of rescue, lifecar, is discussed later.

The description of the rigging of the equipment is much more complicated than the actual work. The service could not afford to have something so complicated that it might confuse or hinder the men when they were tired and working under a strain. The knot used to secure the whip and hawser to the ship's spar was a round turn and two half-hitches. A simple knot to tie, it holds well under a strain and can be tied very rapidly by any sailor on a ship. And the various activities described above were taking place almost simultaneously. While the keeper was aiming the Lyle gun, for instance, part of the crew was burying the sand anchor and other men were arranging the lines.

The lines, blocks, Lyle gun, lanterns, and other equipment were stowed aboard a cart, known as a beach cart or mortar cart, that was kept in a station's boat room ready for use. The wheels of the cart were wide and made of metal, which prevented them from sinking too deeply into the soft sand of a beach. The cart could be pulled by the surfmen or hitched to a team of horses. The cart, and all of the equipment, came

Lyle gun is shot, and projectile and shotline fly toward drill pole. (Coast Guard Museum Northwest)

to be called the beach apparatus by the lifesavers. Fully loaded, the cart weighed close to a thousand pounds.

The surfman's daily routine at stations included seemingly endless drills with the line-throwing rescue equipment. Regulations required the men to exercise with the equipment each Monday and Thursday. The lifesaving crew had to completely rig all of the gear, including actually firing the Lyle gun, within five minutes. The target was a drill pole shaped like a ship's mast that was part of every station. If a drill could not be completed within the allotted time, the man, or men, slowing down the practice could be dismissed from the service.[10]

Repeated drills with the beach apparatus paid dividends. Trained surfmen could set up the apparatus quickly and with little confusion. Drills also built a healthy confidence factor, which was vital. On a stormy night, with the surf pounding on the beach, the temperature hovering near the freezing point, and the shotline fouled, it took great self-discipline and confidence to calmly retrieve the equipment and start over again. The nearly automatic performance of duty could be crucial, especially if the men were tired, wet, and cold from earlier work.

Once the hawser was established between ship and shore, the rescuers could bring two other pieces of equipment into use: the breeches buoy and the lifecar, or surfcar.

Made of galvanized sheet iron, the lifecar was eleven feet four inches

Two crewmen (right) bury sand anchor while other lifesavers lay out lines. (U.S. Coast Guard)

long, four feet eight inches wide, and three feet deep. It weighed 225 pounds, had a rubber fender longitudinally along each gunwale, and resembled an enclosed boat.

Two semicircular bails were attached to the gunwale about one-third the length of the car on each side and extended above the car. At the center of the bail a ring was attached to the hawser. The shipwrecked sailors entered the car through a hatch in the top. Up to eleven people could get into the car. Eleven people would be cramped in the small lifecar, but as one old surfman put it, "Men in that extremity are not apt to stand on the order of their going."[11] Once rigged, the lifecar could be pulled over, upon, or even under the waves.

The lifecar became the topic of a heated debate between Captain Ot-

tinger, who tested lifesaving equipment for the service, and Joseph Francis, owner of the Novelty Iron Works and a builder of metal surfboats. The debate continues today among the few people who study rescue devices. While testing the Manby mortar, Captain Ottinger saw the need for an enclosed device to transport shipwrecked victims. Ottinger approached Joseph Francis with a plan for a surfcar. Francis dutifully built the device. Ottinger declined any patent rights. Francis later went on to form the Francis Life-Boat Company and soon, in the interest of increasing his business, claimed the credit for the invention of the *lifecar*. Ottinger claimed to have invented the *surfcar*. In the final analysis, as Bennett has pointed out, the "differences between the Francis lifecar and the Ottinger surfcar were so insignificant that it would require a patent

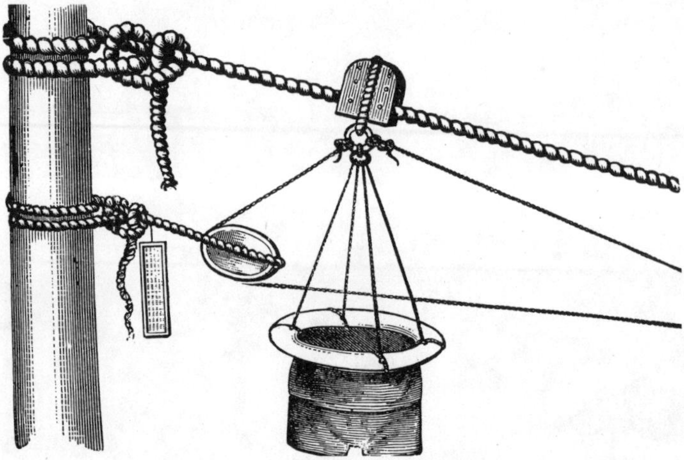

Breeches buoy at the mast with tally board on lower block. Knots are simple round turn and two half-hitches, which hold well under strain. (*Annual Report of the U.S. Life-Saving Service,* 1880)

attorney to tell them apart." The debate has helped to dull the fame of the only lifesaving device wholly developed by Americans during the volunteer era.[12]

The lifecar, or surfcar, began to fall out of favor by the late 1880s. One simple explanation for this is the matter of weight. Everything needed to rig a breeches buoy could be carried on one cart and pulled by the lifesaving crew. To use the lifecar, the rescuers needed two carts:

Cart loaded with breeches buoy equipment was sometimes pulled by horse. (San Francisco Maritime National Historical Park)

Wide wheels on beach apparatus cart were to prevent it from sinking too deeply into sandy beaches. (U.S. Coast Guard)

one just for the device, one for the lines, gun, and other apparatuses. Most U.S. Life-Saving Service Stations were crewed by no more than seven men and using two carts spread the surfmen too thinly.

The development of better navigational equipment and ships that no longer relied on wind power made groundings close to the beach a rare event, thus eliminating the need for the beach apparatus. But the advent

Fully rigged breeches buoy (with passenger) at drill. (From the Jesse Besser Museum Collection, Alpena, Michigan)

Rescue of crew of the ferry *Pere Marquette 3* by lifesavers from Ludington, Michigan, Station. (Weckler Collection, Michigan Maritime Museum, South Haven, Michigan)

Lifecar being hauled out on a hawser. (U.S. Coast Guard)

of the helicopter as a rescue tool was the primary reason for abandoning the use of beach carts. Helicopters can arrive at a wreck site and pluck distressed sailors from a ship quicker than a ground crew could accomplish a breeches buoy rescue. The use of the beach cart did not, however, disappear overnight. As late as the 1960s, the U.S. Coast Guard still trained their small-boat station crews on the Great Lakes with the equipment.[13]

Today one can see beach apparatus drills performed at a few maritime parks. John Krisko, while in charge of the beach cart demonstration at the National Park Service's restored U.S. Life-Saving Service Station at

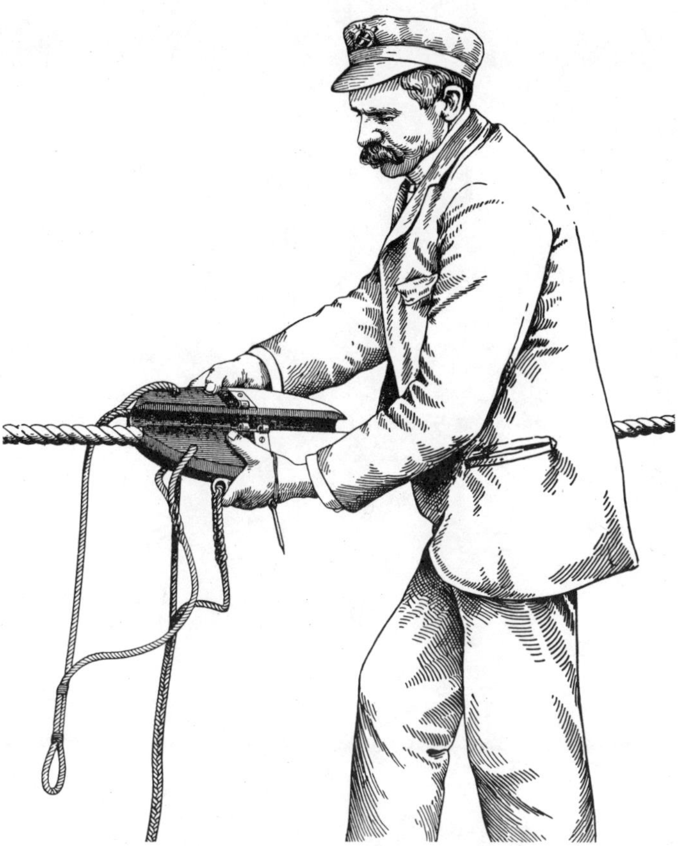

After rescue by breeches buoy or lifecar, a device was sent out on the line to cut the hawser. (*Annual Report of the U.S. Life-Saving Service,* 1880)

Sandy Hook, New Jersey, said, "It took us 20 minutes to do the . . . [beach cart] drill on a still, hot summer day as compared . . . [to the five] minutes during its hey day. Hauling the beach cart through 500 feet of loose sand was about my endurance limit. . . . Executing the drill increases admiration of, and appreciation for, the brave men of the Life Saving Service."[14]

CHAPTER SEVEN

Life at a U.S. Life-Saving Service Station

In their day, the crews of the U.S. Life-Saving Service were pictured by the press and popular magazines as romantic heroes fighting raging surf and howling gales to perform heroic rescues. Many accounts presented a picture of camaraderie, with men lounging about a station just waiting to spring into action. The reality of life at a U.S. Life-Saving Service station was a far cry from this idyllic portrait. The daily routine at a station can be broken into two large segments: official duty and off-duty hours. During official duty the lifesaver's hours were divided between drill and patrol, or lookout, duties. Life at a station can be summed up very simply: hours and hours of boring routine, with always a chance for minutes of sheer terror.

One reason for the success of the U.S. Life-Saving Service was the systematic routine devised for the stations. The service placed great emphasis on drilling (practicing) with rescue equipment and honing other skills. Regulations stated that each day except Sunday some type of regularly scheduled activity would take place. Drills were required to be entered into the station's log book, thus headquarters could check to see if the regulations were being followed.[1]

Crewmen at Neah Bay, Washington. (Coast Guard Museum Northwest)

The beach apparatus was the most complicated rescue gear in the lifesaver's arsenal. Mondays and Thursdays were devoted to working with the beach apparatus, including the actual firing of the Lyle gun. Each station had a drill pole, usually shaped like a ship's mast, which was the practice target. The drill began when the keeper gave the command "Action!" and ended when a crewman was brought down from the drill pole by the breeches buoy. When the district inspector tested the crew the entire routine had to be completed within five minutes. If the drill was not completed within the allotted time, the men slowing down the drill could be dismissed from the service. The emphasis on speed built up a sense of competitiveness between stations, and each unit tried to better its rivals. Sumner I. Kimball wrote that he had personally timed the completion of a drill in two minutes and thirty seconds. He did not indicate, however, whether this drill was accomplished by a regular crew or one specially trained for an exhibition. The roar and smoke of the Lyle gun, the playing out of the shotline, the rigging of the apparatus, and the final pulling of the breeches buoy was always a popular event for the local population to witness.[2]

Rescue by small boat was the least complicated method of bringing shipwrecked sailors to safety, but it was also the most dangerous. The first danger to the lifesavers was the power of high, pounding surf. Station crews often set out into waves that were higher than the length of their rescue boats. Another danger came during the actual moment

Beach apparatus drills usually drew large crowds. Point Arena, California, Station used tree snag for drill pole. (U.S. Coast Guard)

of rescue. Maneuvering a pitching, rolling craft alongside a larger vessel, with broken spars, lines, and other debris nearby, required great skill in boatmanship and the ability to think fast and improvise. One can imagine the desperation of shipwrecked sailors who knew they would die if they did not quickly abandon their ships. If there was a lack of discipline, panic, or a language problem, the sailors aboard a wreck were apt to leap haphazardly into the small heaving boat, with catastrophic results. The entire crew of the Italian ship *Nuova Ottavia,* when wrecked off the

Outer Banks in 1876, panicked and leaped en masse into the surfboat, causing the death of the crew and all the lifesavers.[3]

The need for U.S. Life-Saving Service crews to be small-boat experts is obvious and the service reserved Tuesdays for boat practice. Lifeboat and lifesaving stations were required to launch the surfboat through the surf and pull at the oars for at least thirty minutes. One part of the boat drill was the deliberate capsizing and righting of the craft to ensure that the lifesavers could react quickly and automatically in the event their boat was overturned in heavy seas. In 1912 Noel T. Methley noted that the constant practice enabled the lifesavers to completely right the surfboat after capsizing in "twenty seconds."[4] The drill was so popular with the public that the lifesavers frequently performed it at special functions. In 1890, for example, a reporter for the Marquette (Michigan) *Mining Journal* wrote that next to the Fourth of July parade the most interesting activity was the lifeboat drill. "The men showed very good rowing form as they sent their heavy boat spinning across the harbor. At a signal they capsized the boat, coming upon the other side and resuming their places once more. The crews capsized it eight times . . . to the repeated cheers of the crowd."[5] How cheerful the crew felt after being dunked into the frigid waters of Lake Superior is not recorded.

Ernest H. Rankin, Sr., recalled Keeper Cleary and his crew practicing with a surfboat when he was a young boy:

Capsizing and righting lifeboat was part of weekly drill. (From the Jesse Besser Museum Collection, Alpena, Michigan)

Crew at Frankfort, Michigan, Station during capsize drill. (Institute for Great Lakes Research, Bowling Green State University)

> Suddenly [the boat] turned and headed directly toward me at a rapid pace! It bore down on me, the crew rowing in perfect rhythm and the captain keeping the boat on course with his long oar. On it came faster and faster, and it seemed as if it would crash into the breakwater right under my feet. . . . When the bow of the boat was within a very few feet of the breakwater . . . the captain gave a sharp command. The crew swung around in their seats, grabbed the oars of the men behind them, "backed-water" and brought the boat to an abrupt stop! It was done in a split second. They then backed away, all, even the captain, with broad grins on their faces.[6]

Boat drill itself could be tricky. Surfman Axel Sandstrom, of the station at Coquille River, Oregon, noted in his diary that during a boat drill "we took a big swell that put our boat right on end. The Captain got slung out of his position and the steering oar broke, so we went home again just a little wet." The keeper at Michigan City, Indiana, recorded: "Surfmen Parsons and Joseph Miller were . . . thrown into the lake [while] stearing [*sic*] the boat."[7]

There was also danger present during boat drill. On 22 September 1886 Keeper Edward M. Nelson and two surfmen of the station at Coquille River, Oregon, were drowned when struck by a rogue wave at the entrance to the river. At Point Reyes, California, two surfmen were crushed to death when a "heavy breaker" flipped their boat during drill on 12 December 1890. Less than three years later, on 1 March 1893, another surfman at the same station was killed in a similar accident during drill.[8]

Half the normal work week was taken up with practicing with boats and beach apparatus. By the end of the active season the drills had undoubtedly become a monotonous routine to the lifesavers. This constant and repetitious routine, however, made the surfmen experts. Along with the natural skills that they brought to their positions, the persistent practice enabled the men to perform their duties automatically. The drills also instilled a sense of confidence. Without the crews' natural skills, their innate courage, and the confidence instilled in them through the drills, some shipwrecked sailors would no doubt have perished. Drill periods, however, did not always go by the book. One keeper logged: "Projectile . . . lost in lake, through the fault of Thomas Armstrong not making shot[line] fast to shot."[9]

In the days before radio transmissions the lifesavers had to be adept at signaling with flags. On Wednesdays the surfmen practiced either wig-wag or flag hoists. Wig-wag usually required a team of four: one surfman with a three-foot-square red flag on a pole, another with a white flag of the same dimensions, a surfman with a telescope to read the sending station, and a fourth member to record the message. Wig-wag was used much like Morse code; the red represented a dash and the white a dot. The flag hoists, like signal flags used on ships today, consisted of internationally recognized flags of different colors, patterns, and shapes to spell out a message. Each flag represented a different letter of the alphabet or a number. T. Michael O'Brien has pointed out that the surfmen became so proficient in signaling that "during the Spanish-American War, many [lifesavers] found themselves in the Army Signal Corps."[10] On Fridays the surfmen learned first aid and "restoring the apparently drowned," or artificial respiration. Saturdays were devoted to cleaning the station and Sundays were rest days.[11]

Kimball convinced Congress that America needed a national lifesaving organization. Ironically, because the service was successful most people looked on the U.S. Life-Saving Service as a local entity. The lifesaving stations were often the only national presence in a community, but because most of the crew members came from the surrounding area, the units were looked on as part of the town, with headquarters in far-off Washington, D.C. The stations became *ours,* not *theirs.* This feeling of local organization was reinforced by the lifesavers' actions. The crew of the Brandon, Oregon, station helped fight a fire in the town. The crew of another station helped two women whose buggy had a broken wheel, and another unit assisted in freeing a mired horse. Many government organizations today have officials whose jobs are to maintain good public

Crewmen of Point Betsie, Michigan, aid a shipwreck victim. (Institute for Great Lakes Research, Bowling Green State University)

relations with the local community. The small crews of the U.S. Life-Saving Service had no need for paid professionals to extol their worth to the local population. It was self-evident.[12]

The crewmen were not, however, admired by everyone in a community, nor were there always harmonious feelings between the local population and the lifesavers. Many of the units were in small, tightly knit towns or settlements. Outsiders in these locations are traditionally viewed with some suspicion, if not disfavor. No doubt the service recognized these facts and tried to accommodate the locals. A series of letters concerning the station at North Manitou Island, Michigan, illustrates this point. The superintendent of the Eleventh Life-Saving District, Nathaniel Robbins, when recommending John Wissel to the keeper's position of the station on North Manitou Island, wrote that Wissel would be "acceptable to his neighbors on the Island." In 1886 Robbins recommended that Keeper Charles Lysaght be transferred from the North Manitou Island station to a new station at White River, Michigan. The superintendent noted that the new station was "located near a colony of fishermen of Irish nationality and have the name of being meddlesome, and disposed to run (so to speak) anything that is not to their liking." Lysaght would,

Wig-wag drill. (Institute for Great Lakes Research, Bowling Green State University)

Lifesaving stations were an integral part of local communities. Crew of Point Arena, California, Station march alongside their boat in local parade. (U.S. Coast Guard)

according to Robbins, be the man to stop any type of interference, but even more important: "Wm. Boardman, who owns a large portion of the Island . . . and lives near the Station, would be better pleased to have some other person as Keeper." In 1896 Robbins was recommending another keeper, Peter Olsen, to be transferred. The superintendent recommended that Olsen be moved because of the "feeling against" him by "deserters, discharged men and others." Robbins went on to state that the hostility was "making life for [Olsen] and [his] family miserable by . . . constant bickering." Despite the generally good relationships the service enjoyed with the local communities, some friction did occur.[13]

The U.S. Life-Saving Service ranked lookout and patrol among the more important duties of the surfmen. All lifeboat and lifesaving stations contained a lookout facility of some type. At some units the post consisted of an enclosed room located on the roof with a clear view of the surrounding water area. Other stations had their lookouts in a tower a short distance from the main buildings; other posts were in small structures on higher ground. The lookout was manned during daylight hours, with the hours of watch determined by the keeper. Some units changed the watch every four hours; at others it was longer. The surfman was expected to alertly scan the water, checking for those in distress and logging the passage of ships. To ensure that the man on watch was awake, the lookout stood for the entire period. Many stations also required that the watch strike a bell marking shipboard time, which is measured in half hour intervals. If the bell did not clang at the appointed time, the surfman knew the keeper would soon be hurrying to the lookout. Falling asleep on lookout duty was a quick way to be removed from the service. Standing and scanning for four hours or more is a difficult duty to describe. Having stood lookout tower watches in a lifeboat station in the U.S. Coast Guard, I can assure the reader that the crushing boredom quickly makes the duty wear very thin. But even lookout duty could prove hazardous. The lookout tower at Sleeping Bear Point, Michigan, was struck by lightning and the surfman on watch killed.[14]

In an age of slow communications and sparse population along the coastal areas, a simple but very workable system was put into place to ensure that wrecked ships would be located: Stations were sited three to five miles apart, with beach patrols conducted between the stations. Ideally, a surfman would start off on his patrol toward another station and meet the patrol from that station at a shed about halfway between the two stations. The men would exchange metal tags with their station numbers embossed on them and start back to their units. The tags would be presented to the keeper to prove that the patrol had been made. If the other surfman did not show up, the lifesaver would continue on down the beach to see if there was a problem. At some stations one surfman would remain in the lookout tower and another would set out down the beach. On his return he would go into the tower and the other beach patrolman would trudge in the opposite direction. As the lifesaving network grew, it was not always possible to locate the stations close together, and in these areas the surfmen were expected to patrol a certain distance in one direction, anywhere from one and a half to five miles. At the end of the patrol beat there was a stake with a watchman's clock key attached. The key was inserted into a clock carried by the patrolman and the markings proved that the surfman had made his rounds. The next patrol would be made in the opposite direction.[15]

Surfmen donned oils and, armed with a lantern, metal chits or a watchman's clock, and Coston signals, set out upon their rounds. The Coston signal was a flarelike device that was fired by striking a plunger and igniting a charge. The signal was used to let the crew of a wreck know they had been spotted and help was on the way. The Coston signal was also used to warn off ships that were too close to the beach. During the active season of 1899 surfmen nationwide warned off 143 ships in danger of running aground.[16]

The idea of walking a moonlit beach might seem like pleasant duty. Along the eastern seaboard, however, much of the active season occurred during the winter months, and walking through gale-whipped snow can be rugged. In the Great Lakes the active season stretched into November, hardly a time for a contemplative walk along the beaches of Lake Superior. Contemporary accounts of the beach patrol speak of the shoreline as "clad with ice" and little more than "pathless deserts in the night." The surfmen were forced to plod "through the soft sand, in spite of flooding tides, bewildering snowfalls, overwhelming winds, and bitter cold." Keeper Quinton Morgan, of the station at Sucker River, Michigan, trained his sled dogs to accompany the beach patrol during foggy weather, the "baying of the hounds serving as a type of ambulatory foghorn." Furthermore, stations rarely had more than eight men and it was not unusual for a patrolman to come in off his watch, lie down for an hour or so, and then be called out to pull at the oars of a boat. If a ship was in distress at two in the morning there was no sleeping in, even if one had gotten off patrol at midnight.[17]

Walking their patrol beats the surfmen were bound to run into some unusual sights and situations. The annual reports of the service are replete

Surfman John Sparrow, of Virginia Beach, Virginia, Station starts off on his rounds. Beach patrol was an important duty of surfmen. (Life-Saving Museum of Virginia, Virginia Beach)

with entries about lifesavers gathering up cargo strewn on the beach from a wreck. Among the more grisly discoveries were bodies that had washed ashore. Many of these unknown victims were buried where they were found. This not unusual practice of coming upon the dead led the old-timers of the Vermillion Point, Michigan, station to concoct a story for a new arrival ready to go out on his first beach patrol.[18]

The novice was told about the ghost of Three Finger Riley. A sailor named Riley, so the story went, had been found frozen in the ice along Lake Superior's shoreline. A surfman had carelessly chopped off one of Riley's fingers while trying to free him from the ice. Thereafter the ghost of Riley walked up and down the beach looking for his missing finger. The old-timers would tell the new man: "Sometimes you [can] hear Riley walking behind you in the darkness . . . and sometimes he [will] reach out his bloody hand and tap you on your . . . shoulder!" A crewman would then lie behind the dunes and add noises to the night no doubt helping to fire the new man's already vivid imagination.

A few patrolmen found the inevitable message-in-the-bottle. In 1881 a surfman from the station at Point Betsie, Michigan, found an empty bottle with a note inside that read:

> October 16, 3 o'clock, on board the *Alpena* . . . she has broke her port [side]wheel; is at mercy of seas; is half full of water; God help us, Capt. Napier washed overboard.
>
> George A. N. Moore
> 856 South Halsted Street
> Chicago, Ill.

The other side of the note said: "The finder of this note will please communicate with my wife and let her know of my death." The steamer *Alpena*'s captain, Nelson Napier, went missing on a voyage from Grand Haven, Michigan, to Chicago, in October 1880.[19] A surfman from the Evanston, Illinois, station found a note in a bottle that stated: "I, Peter Knowlton, of New York City, having taken a rowboat from near Van Buren Street on Monday to fish, have been caught in a storm."[20]

Surfmen trudging the beaches had to put up with problems caused by mother nature and human nature. Two patrolmen from the station at Sandy Point were fired upon. Men at stations located near communities of any size were more apt to run into human problems than their fellow lifesavers in more isolated regions. During the 1902–3 season a beach patrolman saved a woman from an assault. One New England surfman carelessly withdrew $172 from the bank before going on duty. When he went into the halfway house, he was attacked. He managed to fight free, only to be assaulted outside by two more attackers, who relieved him of his money. Two muggers near the Evanston Station who encountered a beach patrolman fared less well. Surfman H. C. Smith fought off two holdup men who attacked him. A newspaper account reported that "both of the footpads were given a severe drubbing and Smith continued his work." Smith was a former member of the Northwestern University football team and one of the "best athletes in Evanston."[21]

Beach patrol was not considered the best duty at a U.S. Life-Saving Service station. Scattered throughout the service's records are suggestions by keepers about how to improve this task. In 1900, the keeper of the station at Muskegon, Michigan, requested the district superintendent to allow the surfmen to ride bicycles on patrol. The superintendent rejected the suggestion, noting that riding would require a "greater part of the surfman's time to control his wheel, on account of the nature of the beach." The 1899 regulations specifically noted that patrols had to be carried out on foot. The keeper of the station at Ocracoke, North Carolina, wrote to his superintendent that the patrols from his unit were four and one-half miles one way and had always been made on horseback. The keeper stated that patrolmen "always walk their horses on the patrol and use the same time as they do when they walk on foot." Because of the isolation of the station, the use of horses allowed the surfmen to report to the station "from 30 to 60 minutes earlier than they could on foot" in case of an emergency and prevented the surfmen from arriving exhausted. One keeper along Lake Michigan is alleged to have said that he would fire anyone stupid enough to walk the entire patrol distance on foot. Other letters echoed the comments of the keeper from Ocracoke, as did the superintendent of the district when he forwarded the letter to Washington, D.C. In this case Kimball bowed to the obvious logic of the arguments and allowed all patrols along the North Carolina coast to be on horseback, but stated that the animals had to be walked, except in an emergency. If this privilege was abused, he wrote, it would be "withdrawn."[22]

Many dramatic rescues accomplished by the U.S. Life-Saving Service began with the beach patrolman rushing into the station to give the alarm of a ship ashore. But in one of the most dramatic rescues, the beach patrolman, Surfman Rasmus S. Midgett, of the station at Gull Shoal, North Carolina, did *not* rush to the station. In the typical laconic style of many keepers the log entry for 18 August 1899 states: "R. S. Midgett, surfman No. 1 on south patrol from 3 A.M. to sunrise. He found a wreck broken to pieces 3 miles south of station and on stern was ten men. He managed to save them all without coming to station to report."[23]

The story begins on the night of 17 August when the 643-ton barkentine *Priscilla,* bound from Baltimore to Rio de Janeiro, ran afoul of the infamous weather off Cape Hatteras. Fourteen people were aboard, including Capt. Benjamin E. Springsteen, his wife, his twelve-year-old son, and an older son who was the first mate. Winds were more than one hundred miles per hour, according to Captain Springsteen, "blowing a hurricane from the northeast, and the seas were running mountain high." Some time after nine P.M. the crew felt the *Priscilla* touch lightly, but it was enough to cause the seas to smash through the cabin skylights and quickly drench everyone below decks. Twenty minutes later the ship again grounded, this time violently and permanently. She was so badly wrecked that Captain Springsteen ordered the third and second mates forward to cut away the port rigging. No sooner had this been done than the masts carried away.

Still there was hope, for no lives had been lost. The captain now ordered all hands on deck as the seas began breaking over the hull "with irresistible fury." Suddenly, as the captain clutched his youngest son in his arms, a huge sea slammed into the ship, tearing the boy from his arms and sweeping his wife, his other son, and the cabin boy overboard. In that split second Captain Springsteen lost his entire family. Fifteen or twenty minutes later the hull split in two. The crew managed to remain on the afterdeck section, calling vainly and desperately for help.

Rasmus Midgett, making the south patrol on horseback from Gull Shoal Station, came riding along the beach and spotted boxes, barrels, and other debris coming ashore. The surf on the beach was so high that it reached the saddle girths of his horse, but the evidence of a wreck urged him on. Peering through the darkness, he spurred his horse along for two miles farther where he reined up and listened. A sound drifted in from the darkness, then another. He had found the wreck. But what could he do? If he rode back to the station, it would take hours to return with help. The ship's crew would surely be dead by the time assistance arrived. Midgett hesitated only long enough to think things through. He then dismounted and waited, timing the waves as they pounded in and then slowly receded. Having gauged them, he ran into the ocean after the receding waves, coming as close to the hulk as he dared, and shouted for the sailors to "jump overboard, one at a time, as the surf ran back, and that he would take care of them." He then ran back before the rushing surf.

To the men of the *Priscilla,* it must have seemed an insane plan, but what other hope was there? Midgett watched the surf, then screamed for the first sailor to jump. Over the sailor went. Rasmus rushed forward, grabbed the man, and dragged him to shore. Seven times he rushed headlong into "the jaws of death." Seven times he escaped with his rescued sailors. Now another dilemma confronted the surfman. Three sailors, including Captain Springsteen, were so badly bruised and exhausted that they were unable to move.

Hesitating only a minute, Surfman Midgett plunged into the water again, fought his way through the pounding waves to the side of the hulk, seized one of the ropes, and pulled himself hand over hand to the deck. "Panting for breath from his . . . exertions," he lay there for a few minutes, trying to catch his breath and rest his aching muscles. Regaining his strength somewhat, he put one of the helpless sailors over his shoulder, slid down the rope into the sea, and fought his way through the flaying surf to shore. Twice more Midgett made his harrowing trips. Captain Springsteen proved extremely difficult, as he weighed at least two hundred pounds. When Midgett was struggling up the beach under this burden, a wave "dashed over them." Midgett dug his toes in and fought to keep upright. Later, he admitted that he thought his "time had come." Finally, all ten surviving crewmen of the *Priscilla* lay panting and shivering on the beach. Midgett headed the seven who could walk toward the station. He gave his coat to Captain Springsteen, who had suffered the worst injuries, and set out to get help. Eventually, all were warming themselves at Gull Shoal Station.

Lt. C. E. Johnston, in accordance with regulations, investigated the wreck and rescue. His report stated that Midgett "doesn't deserve any special mention" for the rescue of the first seven sailors, as the men, to some degree, were able to help themselves. Lieutenant Johnston admitted it "was a hazardous piece of work," but Midgett was "an old hand at his business." The rescue of the remaining three crewmen, however, was "quite a different matter." Surfman Rasmus Midgett received the Gold Life Saving Medal.

Beach patrols were discontinued just before World War II. They were reactivated during the war, mostly to detect enemy agents. Patrols were stopped permanently after 1945.[24]

The last aspect of official duty at a lifesaving station entailed miscellaneous duties and cooking. Surfmen had to perform a myriad of tasks to maintain the station and its rescue equipment. Station log books contain numerous entries about crews "cutting wood" and performing "various

Surfman Rasmus S. Midgett won Gold Life Saving Medal for single-handedly rescuing ten people from the *Priscilla,* wrecked along the Outer Banks in 1899. (National Archives)

other odd jobs around the Station." In 1885 surfmen were required to report on and collect marine biological and zoological specimens. The lifesavers reported some unusual and interesting sightings. What caught the attention of the press, however, was a report of a sea serpent. Four members of the station at Sandy Hook, New Jersey, "who had only pork, potatoes, and water for dinner," and were reported to be "honest, temperate, and apparently truthful men," claimed to have sighted a creature of at least three hundred feet in length and were "certain" it was not a whale.[25]

There was no rating for cook, so the men either shared the duty, appointed one man to undertake the task for the entire season, or hired a woman to do the kitchen chores. Some accounts detail fairly good meals. If the cooking was done on a rotational basis, duty usually ran from noon to noon, with the surfman responsible for the preparation of the meals and the cleanliness of the galley. One old salt, who served along the shores of Lake Superior, remembered that at Deer Park, Michigan, the cook shack was located away from the main building to prevent any chance of fire destroying this isolated station. Former surfman John F. Soldenski recalled that the mess cook shack and mess cabin was a "shoddily-built affair, drafty and poorly insulated. . . . During the summer, spaces between the . . . boards offered an open invitation to the myriads of mosquitoes and black flies; these likewise made meals short."[26]

The relationships between the crewmen themselves was another aspect of life at a lifesaving station. The few writers who have written about the service imply that because crews worked as teams the surfmen were a close-knit family. In fact, the perfection in working with rescue equipment was the result of constant drills and natural abilities. Many outsiders, however, saw this teamwork as camaraderie. There is some truth in this, but there is also another side to how the men interacted.

A strict interpretation of the service's regulations reveals the men were to remain on duty constantly, but could, at the discretion of the keeper, be allowed one day off, weather permitting. Even then the surfman had to remain within communication distance of the station. Furthermore, some keepers tended to rule their units with all the authority of an old-time sailing ship captain. Mixing monotonous routine, long duty days, isolation, and strong authority can produce an explosive concoction. Buried within the service's annual reports and in the station logs are indications that not all crews worked cheerfully together. The station at Bolinas Bay, California, was apparently torched by a disgruntled former crewman. Keeper Morgan kept a pistol at hand because his crew had threatened him. The inspector of the Eleventh District reported that one keeper treated his men badly.[27] In the 1898 log book of the station at Michigan City, Indiana, the keeper wrote: "Charles Allen very slovenly in make up of his bed. Very rare it is made up neatly." This is the beginning of a running dispute between the keeper and Allen. Soon Allen is reported as "using bad language," "being saucy," and threatening to "fix Keeper first chance he got." The surfman embarked on a destructive rampage, breaking first a spittoon, next a window, and finally with great effort a grindstone. In a bit of understatement, the keeper reports that Allen has a "violent temper." Finally Allen "fires 3 shots in [the] sitting room." This latest incident apparently exhausted the keeper's patience, for his entry in the log a few days after the shooting incident indicates that Allen has been suspended for "being Malicious, Revengeful, destructive and not pay[ing] his bills." The stations of the U.S. Life-Saving Service were not, however, all seething masses of discontent. Many units were not only well disciplined, but were also cheerful places to serve, and the crews did enjoy a very close camaraderie. The interaction of the crews of the U.S. Life-Saving Service was like that of any other organization made up of human beings: a complicated mix of both good and bad.[28]

Another important aspect of living at a U.S. Life-Saving Service station was off-duty activities and family life. When not pursuing official duties the surfmen were free to undertake off-duty activities. Some men worked on crafts such as making chairs; others made traditional sailor fancy work; other surfmen simply played checkers and cards. At one station, however, the keeper forbade card playing because it was the "devil's activity." Books were donated to the U.S. Life-Saving Service and distributed to some of the more isolated stations. Almost all contemporary accounts that mention the lifesavers' off-duty life state that they were great tellers of sea stories.[29]

To help supplement their diet and provide an off-duty activity, surfmen fished, farmed, and hunted. There is evidence that, unbeknownst to headquarters, the men at some stations actually turned a profit in these activities, as one surfman's letter stated: "We have been fishing . . . [for] two days. . . . We got 1,660 fish. . . . Today we got about 250 so we have caught quite a lot of fish this week. Don't tell anyone about this." A

Furnishings at most stations were rather Spartan. (Life-Saving Museum of Virginia, Virginia Beach)

Lifesavers found various means of filling the long hours between rescues. (Institute for Great Lakes Research, Bowling Green State University)

Lyle gun projectiles are neatly stowed (upper right) in boathouse of West Coast station. Ship nameboards (far right) are probably from a wreck. (Coast Guard Museum Northwest)

North Carolina nimrod-keeper was dismissed for his excessive waterfowl hunting and for using government powder for shooting. At another station, a surfman made furniture on his off-duty time to sell.[30]

The long stretch of duty days and isolation could cause problems for single men and keepers. In 1874 the keeper of the station at Squan Beach, New Jersey, became embroiled with headquarters because the U.S. Army Signal Corps sergeant attached to the station was caught sleeping with a woman of "ill fame" at the station.[31] The station at Evanston, Illinois, located on the grounds of Northwestern University and crewed by students, had difficulties not encountered by many other units. In 1900, the Chicago *Tribune* reported that Keeper Lawrence O. Lawson feared his surfmen were not keeping their minds strictly on their duties because "every afternoon, before and after drill, the members are surrounded by bevies of fair maids, and in the evening the lake shore is dotted with groups of young women talking to the lifesavers. Even when it is time for their favorites to go on patrol duty the young women do not depart, but turn their attention to the reserve men."[32]

Family life was also difficult for the married lifesavers. Long duty days meant separation for at least six days of the week. Surfman Sandstrom's diary noted a series of burglaries near his home, some forty miles distant from the station, and related that his wife was "scared and I do not blame her. I wish that I could be at home."[33] At isolated units, however, the hardships became even greater. Some stations were so remote that it was impossible for a surfman to visit regularly with his family. At the Sucker River, Michigan, unit, it was a two-day walk to the nearest settlement of any size. Only the keeper's family was officially allowed to reside in the station proper. At many isolated stations, surfmen built houses for their families either on the property of the unit or nearby. Some of the structures were little more than log cabins; others were more polished buildings. Along Lake Superior small communities grew up beside some of the stations, as many of the married lifesavers chose to live nearby instead of moving out at the end of the active season.[34]

The close proximity of women to isolated men could cause problems. The Providence (Rhode Island) *Journal* reported that Surfman Fred Frenzen, of the station at Highland, Massachusetts, had been wounded by surfman Arthur Lombard with buckshot in the leg, abdomen, and face while on patrol. Surfman Frenzen had drawn a pistol and returned fire, missing with all five shots. Why had this wild West shootout taken place along Cape Cod's beaches, and why was a surfman carrying a pistol on patrol? According to the *Journal,* Surfman Frenzen

Like sailors everywhere, the lifesavers were not adverse to visits from members of the opposite sex. Some of the women have donned cork lifejackets. (Michigan Maritime Museum, South Haven, Michigan)

was concerned about Surfman Lombard's "objectionable attentions to Mrs. Frenzen."[35]

Life for wives and children at the remote stations was difficult. The families had limited contact with people, and the opportunities for cultural activities were severely limited. Keeper Jason F. Pratton's letter to the superintendent of the Eleventh District reflects what many married lifesavers faced. Pratton wrote that he needed to move because "my family must have Schooling." In some island communities along the eastern seaboard, however, schools were provided for the children, whereas at others a woman undertook the task of teaching the children. For some educated women the isolation must have been a strain. Keeper John Parsons's wife, living on isolated Thunder Bay Island, Michigan had a college education and had taught music.[36]

Wives were all too aware that when their husbands pushed out into the surf they might not return. At the Vermillion Station, when the crew set out into Lake Superior, the women "would build a large fire on the

This sign at the station at Point Betsie, Michigan, probably reflects the feelings of many lifesavers. (National Park Service Photograph)

beach and pray for their [husbands'] return."[37] The families also faced danger because of lack of medical care. According to former Surfman Soldenski, in a cemetery near the now abandoned station at Two Hearted River, Michigan, lie a surfman, and the wife of Keeper Albert Ocha and several of their children.[38]

The history of the U.S. Life-Saving Service is dominated by the heroic rescues of its crewmen. Many people do not realize that women are also a part of this legacy. At Point Lookout, Long Island, for example, a

The small buildings (left) outside the station's fence line belonged to married lifesavers. Only the keeper's family could reside in the unit, so married crewmen built their own houses. (U.S. Coast Guard)

Married lifesavers and their families endured isolation. Two of the children are dressed as lifesavers: one wears oilskins and cork lifebelt, the other a miniature keeper's uniform. (Michigan Maritime Museum, South Haven, Michigan)

vessel wrecked nearby during the inactive season. Three women who were guests of the keeper's wife helped in rescuing twelve sailors. Across the continent, at Humboldt Bay, California, the keeper's wife and two other women assisted in a rescue. On the Gulf of Mexico, again during the inactive season, the Norwegian bark *Catharine* grounded during a hurricane. The "breakers ran so high" that the beach apparatus, one of the more complicated pieces of equipment used by the lifesavers, was brought into use. The keeper's two daughters, Sara Louise and Visa Broadbent, assisted in rescuing the entire crew. For their work, Sara Louise and Visa received a gold medal from the King of Sweden. Probably the most notable of all the women who assisted the lifesavers in their work was Edith Morgan, of Hamlin, Michigan.[39]

On 23 March 1878, before the opening of the active season, a strong northerly gale struck northern Lake Michigan. The bitterly cold wind quickly whipped up pounding waves. An overturned small boat was spotted three miles from shore, with two men clinging desperately to it. The nearest U.S. Life-Saving Service unit was Grand Point au Sable, where Keeper Sanford W. Morgan was in charge. The only people available to assist Keeper Morgan were his two sons, one of whom was a boy, and his daughter, Edith. Keeper Morgan realized his family could not row the surfboat in such a storm, so he opted to use a small fishboat.

Morgan put his youngest son at the sweep oar to steer the small boat, while he, Edith, and the other son pulled oars. To reach the capsized boat the family of rescuers would have to cross two bars, over which the waves were breaking heavily. The U.S. Life-Saving Service's official report notes that Edith "did her part in the hard work which followed," but with such a small craft the boat barely made it over the first bar, and by the time the would-be rescuers reached the second bar the boat "was nearly swamped." Keeper Morgan decided to put about. Upon reaching the beach he immediately dispatched his older son, James, to town to gather a volunteer crew and return with the surfboat. Meanwhile father and daughter began to clear a path for the surfboat "through a great mass of logs and driftwood" that covered the beach. Edith and her father worked "with such energy" that when the crew arrived the way was clear for the launching of the boat. Edith helped in ramming the surfboat into the waves and eventually the two men were brought to safety. Just before Christmas of 1879, again during the inactive season, Edith once more proved her courage.[40]

On 21 December 1879 the steamer *The City of Toledo* grounded two hundred to three hundred yards offshore in a gale-whipped snowstorm. The ship swung and lay broached in ten feet of water, with seas breaking over her. The weather was bitterly cold. The waters sweeping over the steamer froze and soon the ship "resembled an iceberg." The steamer struck between the units at Grand Point au Sable and Ludington. The keeper of the Ludington station set out with volunteers and the surfboat.

The first problem facing the rescuers were high banks of ice rafted upon the beach. At last the boat was launched, but the cold weather was so severe that the thole pins clogged with ice, preventing the use of oars. Meanwhile, Keeper Morgan had assembled some volunteers and started to the wreck site with the beach apparatus. Edith was among the volunteers.

Once this group arrived, a line was quickly established to the grounded ship by the Lyle gun, but the cold weather again hampered the rescue. Ice clogged the tackle and lines, making the process painfully slow. Edith, along with the other volunteers, stood in the piercing wind, in fifteen inches of snow for five or six hours working the apparatus. Keeper Morgan decided to set out in the surfboat, and eventually everyone on *The City of Toledo* was brought safely ashore. For her heroic work on these two occasions Edith Morgan received the Silver Life Saving Medal, the service's second-highest award.

Life at a U.S. Life-Saving Service station consisted of long hours of monotonous official duties, such as practicing with rescue equipment and trudging along the shoreline on beach patrol. Time on duty was long, generally six days a week. A large part of a lifesaver's day, however, was taken up in off-duty pursuits. To while away the hours before going on duty, the men engaged in such activities as fishing, hunting, making crafts, playing cards and checkers, or simply swapping sea stories. In some of the isolated units, the families of the lifesavers shared the hardships of the crewmen. Only the family of the keeper was allowed to live in the station itself; the other married families had to construct living quarters on or near the station themselves. No housing allowance was given to the surfmen. Living in isolated regions, far from medical care, the wives and children shared the dangers and worries of the lifesavers. Contrary to the popular press of the day, life at a U.S. Life-Saving Service station did not consist of idly waiting around for exciting adventures, but of long hours of official duties and longer hours of filling in the time between these duties. But the lifesavers never knew when these long hours of boredom would be broken by minutes of sheer terror as they attempted a rescue in high surf and howling gale.

CHAPTER EIGHT

Eight Bells

As the twentieth century began, Sumner I. Kimball had been at the helm of the U.S. Life-Saving Service nearly thirty years. Kimball must have been pleased with his efforts to create a professional, nationwide lifesaving service. His crews received favorable publicity and were looked upon as heroes by many. True, there were some disappointments, such as low pay and no retirement system, but with time these difficulties could, perhaps, be ironed out. All in all, the organization that Kimball led had a reputation for being well run, thrifty, and humanitarian. Less than two decades later, on 15 January 1915, the U.S. Life-Saving Service ceased to exist. By 1940 most people had never heard of the service. Three broad waves of change that converged in the first fifteen years of the twentieth century brought about this dramatic reversal and overwhelmed the organization.

Improved marine technology shaped one of the currents of change. The few aids to navigation available in this country were of dubious quality. In 1852, 333 lighthouses dotted the U.S. coastline. Until the late 1850s, the primary illuminate for the lights was whale oil in a lantern with a wick.[1] The best lighthouses were those in which the keeper kept the lantern's wick nicely trimmed. (The amount of time spent trimming these wicks earned all lighthouse keepers the sobriquet "wickie.") When

Kimball began reorganizing the lifesaving network in 1871, ships were made of wood and were powered by the wind. The approaches to New York City, the busiest port in nineteenth-century United States, contained many sandbars, and the chance of strong nor'easters driving sailing ships onto these submerged hazards was high. Seafarers entering the gateway to the United States faced the danger of running aground because of capricious winds and poor navigational aids.

The U.S. Life-Saving Service's rescue procedures reflected the technology of the 1870s. Most rescue attempts involved commercial, wooden sailing vessels that were coasting, and the wreck usually lay close to the beach. The means of detecting and responding to those in distress were, of necessity, unsophisticated. Surfmen patrolling the beach or scanning the sea from a lookout post were the primary means of locating wrecks. The lifesaver's arsenal consisted of oar-powered small boats or a line-throwing gun. One unwritten (and unenforceable) premise was that the crew would only have to handle one wreck per day or night. On the occasions when more than one rescue attempt occurred in a single day or night, the log books and annual reports clearly indicate that the lifesavers were nearly overwhelmed. What usually saved the day in these cases was the help of volunteers.

By 1900 maritime technology had advanced to the stage that ships were built of steel and were machine-powered. No longer were vessels completely at the mercy of the winds. Navigational equipment and aids to navigation in the United States had improved. By 1913 the number of lighthouses had increased to 1,462, and kerosene was the illuminate, with electricity slowly being introduced. Ships were able to stay further offshore and were less likely to run aground.[2]

Improved technology actually created serious problems for the U.S. Life-Saving Service. Launching small oar-powered boats to rescue vessels stranded close to the beach was dangerous, but usually entailed a relatively short period of time. Once ships were able to navigate further offshore, the danger and time involved in rowing to a ship increased, especially in a storm-tossed sea.

As the nature of deep-water shipping was changing, another technological improvement had a significant impact on the service. The U.S. Life-Saving Service's 1909 annual report noted that "a new element in navigation . . . has in a remarkable degree increased . . . duties and notably added to the annual statistical showing. This new feature is the gasoline motor boat."[3] At about the time machine-powered boats began to be seen, recreational boating increased. Not only did this mean more boats in the coastal waters, but in many cases the craft were piloted by people with very little nautical skill. Inevitably all of this combined to create situations in which more than one boat at a time needed assistance. But the U.S. Life-Saving Service was equipped to handle only one rescue at a time. The number of small boats needing assistance stretched the resources of the service. As long as the U.S. Life-Saving Service continued to rely on the technology of the 1870s, it was being passed by. The service needed improved boats and larger crew size. Kimball began to shift to motorized boats by 1905. Eight years later, 70 motor lifeboats and 60 power surfboats were in operation, and in the final year of the service the numbers had increased to 80 lifeboats and 150 surfboats.[4] Kimball recognized the need for improved rescue boats, but the changes came slowly.

In the meantime the second major factor in the demise of the service was being felt: inadequate pay and no retirement system for the U.S. Life-Saving Service. People will sometimes work for low pay, especially if they feel they are contributing to a worthwhile enterprise or if no other employment is available. Inadequate salaries, therefore, were not as important as the lack of a retirement system. Without a pension system, men often stayed in a position until they died or were forced to resign for physical disabilities. As a result advancement opportunities in the service were limited. Put simply, the organization was growing old. Robert F. Bennett notes that by 1915 there were "keepers in their seventies manning the customary sweep oar while the strokes were manned by men in their sixties."[5] Rescue work requires stamina and agility. (Kimball had also aged. In 1900, at the age of sixty-six, he was still in command of the service and no move was made to replace him with another general superintendent.) The lack of a pension system was not because Kimball did not try. He made numerous efforts to establish a retirement system for the lifesavers, all of which failed. Increased technology and lack of a pension system were two strong waves eroding the strength of the U.S. Life-Saving Service. But the third wave was about to overwhelm it.

President William Howard Taft said that the huge industrial growth in the United States came through the "use of the principle of organization and combination and through the development of our natural resources." He went on to remark that in the process of developing the capital to build the industries "we nearly transferred complete political power to those who controlled corporate wealth and we were in danger of a plutocracy."[6] The concern over a plutocracy was one reason for a reform political force known as the Progressive Movement. Progressives, who were drawn from both political parties, sought to redress the excesses of runaway growth. Social reform, such as shorter work hours, child labor laws, and woman's suffrage, were pushed by the Progressives. Political reform was also on the agenda. There was a strong push to democratize the government and make the legislature more responsive to the people.[7]

The national government, of course, came under scrutiny. Following his views of "organization and combination," President Taft, under acts of 25 June 1910 and 3 March 1911, appointed a commission to find ways to improve the economy and efficiency of the federal government. Frederick A. Cleveland, an economist and financial adviser to the president, headed what became known as the Taft Commission. The various small maritime police and safety forces of the federal government were one of the areas to come under close examination.

From its inception the U.S. Life-Saving Service was part of the Treasury Department. The U.S. Lighthouse Service, founded in 1789, whose function was to provide aids to navigation, was part of the same department. Another small organization in Treasury was the Steamboat Inspection Service, founded in 1838; its mission was to ensure that the propulsion machinery aboard ships was in safe condition. The most complex maritime organization in the Treasury Department was the U.S. Revenue Cutter Service (USRCS), founded in 1790 and originally called the U.S. Revenue Marine. The USRCS had a multiplicity of duties. Although it provided rescue services on the high seas, it was actually established to help prevent smuggling into the fledgling United States. Over the years it acquired other law enforcement duties, ranging from quarantine enforcement to stopping the poaching of fur seals in the Bering Sea. The service evolved into a uniformed maritime police and safety force, with military duties in times of war. It had fought in all the major naval engagements of the United States and had commissioned officers. By the beginning of the twentieth century the organization had a training school and, by 1906, a retirement system. Periodically the U.S. Navy had tried unsuccessfully to take over the USRCS. In 1903 the Steamboat Inspection Service and the Lighthouse Service were transferred to the Department of Commerce and Labor and ten years later were shuffled to the newly created Commerce Department, leaving only the USRCS and the U.S. Life-Saving Service within the Treasury Department. In 1911 these maritime police and safety forces were about to come under the Taft Commission's scrutiny.[8]

The commission found similarities between the Life-Saving Service and Lighthouse Service. Many of the U.S. Life-Saving Service's stations were located near lighthouses and the two services maintained similar administrative organizations. The commission also felt that both entities' basic duty was to protect life and property along the coastline of the United States. To counter this perceived duplication of effort, the commission recommended that the U.S. Life-Saving Service be discontinued and the operation of its stations be made a part of the Bureau of Lighthouses in the Department of Commerce. The savings realized by this change would amount to approximately $150,000.[9] Oliver M. Maxam, assistant general superintendent of the U.S. Life-Saving Service, filed a minority report. Maxam agreed that stations of both services were located near each other and that both organizations helped mariners, but there the similarities ended. Lighthouses, he wrote, are "fixed agencies requiring the constant, undivided, and vigilant attention of their keepers and crews on the spot." Lifesaving stations, on the other hand, are "merely the headquarters of the crews, whose duties require them to go wherever their services may be needed at wrecks and also to patrol the beaches and maintain watches for the early discovery of wrecks and the hastening of relief." Qualifications for employment in the two organizations were far different. A lifesaver, for example, had to be an expert boatman; this was not necessary for duty at a lighthouse. Maxam noted that the commission did not mention the close arrangement with another organization, the USRCS. Officers of the USRCS had been detailed to the U.S. Life-Saving Service since its beginnings. Despite Maxam's arguments, President Taft accepted the commission's findings and on 4 April 1912 recommended that Congress pass the legislation necessary to carry out the proposed merger.

The harshest verdict fell upon the USRCS. The commission felt "that the service has not a single duty or function that cannot be performed by some existing service, and be performed by the latter at much smaller expense on its part." It recommended that the service be abolished, with its duties and cutters spread about the federal government. The disbanding of the USRCS would realize a savings of at least $1 million for each year the organization was abolished.

The commission also suggested that the three departments most affected by the recommendations—Commerce and Labor, Treasury, and the Navy—submit their views. As might be expected, Secretary Charles Nagel, of Commerce and Labor, was agreeable to the mergers and saw nothing wrong with abolishing the USRCS, as many of the cutters would probably come to his department.

George von L. Meyer, Secretary of the Navy, saw both advantages and disadvantages to abolishing the USRCS. One disadvantage was that the Navy would find itself doing many of the police duties of the USRCS, and the secretary pointed out that all "duties which interfere with the training of personnel for war are irregular and in a degree detrimental to the efficiency of the fleet." The Navy, however, would welcome the addition of the small cutters to the fleet, as well as the USRCS's enlisted men. The officer corps was another matter. The secretary felt the officers "would be of no possible advantage to the Navy, but a serious menace to the harmony of the personnel."

Not unexpectedly, Secretary of the Treasury Franklin MacVeagh lashed out at the commission. Writing that the recommendation to abolish the USRCS had come "out of a clear sky," he questioned the commission's assertion that monetary savings would result from its recommendation. Despite MacVeagh's appeals and numerous statistics provided by the USRCS, President Taft agreed with the commission and recommended abolishing the service. Buried within the report that the president transmitted to Congress were some interesting comments.

Secretary Nagel offered as an alternative to the commission's report a plan to create a federal maritime safety and law enforcement agency made up of the Light House Service, the Life-Saving Service, and the USRCS. MacVeagh had a less ambitious program. He wrote that it "might be very well to make the Life-Saving Service a part of the Revenue Cutter Service, and I believe that will be done." While this maneuvering was taking place, political events overtook the president. Taft found himself estranged from parts of his own party and leading an administration that had a dubious chance of remaining in office. This gave MacVeagh very little time to implement any sort of merger. Nevertheless, he ordered the captain commandant of the USRCS, Ellsworth P. Bertholf, to work out a plan to combine the two organizations. Kimball and Bertholf hammered out a plan, but the Taft administration was replaced by that of Woodrow Wilson. Another two years passed before final action could be taken. On 19 December 1914 President Wilson sent a letter to Congressman Oscar W. Underwood expressing his "very great interest in the bill which has been passed by the Senate and is pending in the House which provides for the consolidation of the Revenue-Cutter Service and Life-Saving Service." Wilson went on to note that the passage of the bill had the "highest consequence for the efficiency of both services." Representative William C. Adamson, of Georgia, steered the bill through the House.

Joshua James, legendary lifesaver, died on active duty at age seventy-four. (U.S. Coast Guard)

The Act to Create the Coast Guard was approved on 20 January 1915, with 212 yeas and 79 nays.[10]

The plans made by Bertholf and Kimball placed the civilian lifesavers within a military organization. District superintendents were made commissioned officers, keepers became warrant officers, and surfmen were entered as enlisted men, with the position of number one surfman rated as a petty officer. Most importantly, by being part of a military organization the lifesavers finally obtained a retirement system. The act that created the U.S. Coast Guard also provided for Kimball's retirement.

Why was Kimball willing to see his organization subsumed within the USRCS? Little documentation on Kimball's decision making exists, but one factor must have been the long association with the Treasury Department. By 1915 Kimball had spent more than half a century within the department. He had been the civilian head of the USRCS, and during his forty-four years in charge of the U.S. Life-Saving Service he had had a close relationship with the USRCS. Kimball would not have been eager

Joshua James's body was placed in a boat for his funeral. (U.S. Coast Guard)

Sumner Increase Kimball, sole head of the U.S. Life-Saving Service and its driving force, remains an obscure figure. (U.S. Coast Guard)

to start over again in another federal department. Equally important, he realized that merging with a military organization would ensure a retirement system for his lifesavers. If the service were to merge with the U.S. Lighthouse Service it would probably not obtain a pension system. In fact, some of the nays recorded against the formation of the U.S. Coast Guard came because a "few Congressmen expressed concern about the expense of extending military retirement benefits to Life-Saving personnel."[11] Kimball's long association with Treasury and the chance to acquire a retirement system for his lifesavers must have seemed like compelling reasons for the merger with the USRCS. Kimball's long service in lifesaving did not end with his retirement. In May 1915 he was appointed president of the Board on Life Saving Appliances. At the time of his appointment he was eighty-one.

Kimball was unquestionably the driving force behind the United States' possessing a first-class lifesaving organization. Much of the present-day Coast Guard's highly regarded reputation as a humanitarian organization is the result of his organizational skills and management abilities. Many of the routines that he established, such as constant drills with rescue equipment, are just as important today as they were more than a century ago.

In the final analysis Kimball was the ultimate bureaucrat: he knew how to work within the federal government. Kimball himself never actively sought the limelight, but he realized that the exploits of his lifesavers were dramatic and could help sway politicians who controlled the purse strings. Hiring William D. O'Connor, a professional author, to write the annual reports shows Kimball's genius at what we would now call public relations. The regulations he passed over the years were designed not only to improve the service, but to remove the crew members from reproach. Kimball realized that to create a professional service, and one that was in large part located in small communities, his crews would have to be above petty politics and be seen as a service to the community and the nation. Apparently Kimball lived his life along the same lines. No taint of scandal ever touched him, and his life-style made him as anonymous as the faceless clerks that served in Washington, D.C. Sumner Increase Kimball died in 1923, in Washington, D.C., with very little notice. He remains obscure. Perhaps it is fitting in some ways that Kimball has not been the subject of the biography he so richly deserves. Many of his former lifesavers lived their lives performing brave deeds and have long been forgotten.

The lifesaving routines of the old U.S. Life-Saving Service remained basically unchanged for many years, but headlines now proclaimed stirring rescues by the U.S. Coast Guard. As the old lifesavers retired their former organization began to fade from the public's mind. By the beginning of World War II most people did not remember the predecessor of the new service. As the U.S. Coast Guard developed better, faster boats and helicopters became an important tool in search and rescue, not as many stations were needed and many of the units were closed. Some of the abandoned buildings were destroyed by vandals; others were put to new uses. The U.S. Life-Saving Service slipped further and further behind the veil of time.

Today the U.S. Life-Saving Service's brave deeds are recalled only at a few maritime museums or national lake- and seashores. The crack of the Lyle gun is no longer heard; it has been replaced by the staccato roar of the helicopter. Gone is the picturesque drama of the keeper standing erect in the stern of the surfboat, urging his crewmen on, their faces contorted with the strain of pulling the plunging boat through the surf. The sweat and straining muscles of the surfmen have been replaced by the whine and exhaust roar of the modern lifeboat engine.

Though never in the mainstream of American life, these brave men of the surf began a long tradition of service to others. As an assistant inspector so aptly wrote: "These . . . men . . . took their lives in their hands, and, at the most imminent risk, crossed the most tumultuous sea . . . , and all for what? That others might live to see homes and friends."

Notes

CHAPTER 1

1. *Annual Report of the Operations of the United States Life-Saving Service for the Fiscal Year Ending June 30, 1902* (Washington, D.C.: U.S. Government Printing Office, 1903): 240–41 (*ARUSLSS*).

2. Unless otherwise noted, all material on the *Taulane* is found in: *ARUSLSS, 1880,* 106–20; William D. O'Connor, *Heroes of the Storm* (Boston: Houghton, Mifflin, 1904), 81–92.

3. Material on the Point aux Barques crew is found in "Journals of the U.S. Life-Saving Service Station," ("Journals") Point aux Barques, Michigan, 23 April 1880, Records of the U.S. Coast Guard (RUSCG), Record Group 26 (RG26), Washington National Records Center (WNRC), Suitland, Md.; *ARUSLSS, 1880,* 21–26.

4. Unless otherwise noted all material, including the quotes by Keeper Matthews, are found in "Journals," Point Betsie, Michigan, 11–13 October 1880, RUSCG, RG26 WNRC; *ARUSLSS, 1881,* 19–36; O'Connor, *Heroes of the Storm,* 93–112; "Scrapbooks," RUSCG, RG26, National Archives.

CHAPTER 2

1. Dennis R. Means, "A Heavy Sea Running: The Formation of the U.S. Life-Saving Service, 1846–1878," *Prologue: Journal of the National Archives,* 19, no. 4 (Winter 1987): 223. The only two in-depth studies on the formation of the U.S. Life-Saving Service are the Means article (note 1) and Robert F. Bennett,

Surfboats, Rockets, and Carronades (Washington, D.C.: U.S. Government Printing Office, 1976). Bennett's work deals primarily with operational matters, while Means's deals with the political machinations of the service. I have relied heavily on these two important works.

2. F. Ross Holland, *America's Lighthouses: Their Illustrated History Since 1716* (Brattleboro, Vt.: Stephen Greene Press, 1972), 32.

3. The hazards of entering New York Harbor are well covered in Bennett, *Surfboats, Rockets, and Carronades,* 14–16.

4. Unless otherwise noted, all material on the *Mexico* is found in Dennis L. Noble and T. Michael O'Brien, "That Others Might Live: The Saga of the U.S. Coast Guard," *American History Illustrated* (June 1976): 5.

5. For the work of the Massachusetts Humane Society, see M. A. DeWolfe Howe, *The Humane Society of the Commonwealth of Massachusetts: An Historical Review, 1785–1916* (Boston: Riverside Press, 1918).

6. Bennett, *Surfboats, Rockets, and Carronades,* 1–2; Senate Committee on Commerce, *W. A. Newell. Letter from the Secretary of the Treasury, Transmitting Report of the General Superintendent of the Life-Saving Service Relative to the Claims of W. A. Newell as the Originator of the System of the Life-Saving Service of the United States,* 55th Cong., 2d Sess., 1898, S.Doc. 270 (*Newell Letter*). Other legislation prior to 1848 dealt with lifesaving. On 3 March 1847 legislation was passed "for rendering assistance from the shore to victims of shipwreck. . . . The allocated funds, however, were not used for their designated purpose but carried forward and in 1849 placed at the disposal of the Massachusetts Humane Society." Means, "Heavy Sea Running," 224.

7. Bennett, *Surfboats, Rockets, and Carronades,* 14–15.

8. Letter, Stephen Pleasonton to Robert J. Walker, 22 August 1848, "Miscellaneous Letters, . . . 1848–56," RUSCG, RG26, National Archives.

9. Means, "Heavy Sea Running," 224.

10. Bennett, *Surfboats, Rockets, and Carronades,* 28–29; Means, "Heavy Sea Running," 225.

11. Means, "Heavy Sea Running," 225.

12. Rebecca Harding Davis, "Life Saving Stations," *Lippincott's Magazine,* 17 (March 1876): 310.

13. Means, "Heavy Sea Running," 226; *ARUSLSS, 1876,* 76.

14. Quoted in Means, "Heavy Sea Running," 227.

15. Ibid.

16. Ibid.

17. Bennett, *Surfboats, Rockets, and Carronades,* 77.

18. Ibid.

19. Ibid.

CHAPTER 3

1. Means, "Heavy Sea Running," 227.

2. Quoted in Means, "Heavy Sea Running," 227.

3. Senate Committee on Commerce, *Letter from the Secretary of the Treasury Communicating . . . The Present Condition of the Life-Saving Stations on the Coasts*

of New Jersey and Long Island, 42d Cong., 2d Sess., 1872, S.Ex.Doc. 22; "Synopsis of Report of Capt. John Faunce on Inspection of Life-Saving Stations on Coasts of Long Island and New Jersey, August 1871"; "Summary of Expenditures Required for New and Old Life-Saving Stations. Coasts of Long Island and New Jersey, September 1871"; "Estimate for Coast of New Jersey, October 12, 1871, John Faunce Captain and Inspector," in "Miscellaneous, 1849–75," Box 1, RUSCG, RG26, National Archives.

4. Dumas Malone, ed., *Dictionary of American Biography,* vol. 13 (New York: Charles Scribner's, 1958), 619–20.

5. O'Connor, *Heroes of the Storm,* xi–xii.

6. Bennett, *Surfboats, Rockets, and Carronades,* 78.

7. Quoted in Bennett, *Surfboats, Rockets, and Carronades,* 77–78.

8. Robert F. Bennett, "The Lifesavers: 'For Those in Peril on the Sea'," U.S. Naval Institute, *Proceedings,* 102 (March 1976): 58.

9. Quoted in Jeannette Edwards Rattray, *Ship Ashore! A Record of Maritime Disasters off Montauk and Eastern Long Island, 1640–1955* (New York: Coward-McCann, 1955), 97.

10. Bennett, "The Lifesavers," 58.

11. Darrell Hevenor Smith and Fred Wilbur Powell, *The Coast Guard: Its History, Activities and Organization* (Washington, D.C.: Brookings Institution, 1929), 35.

12. Bennett, "The Lifesavers," 59.

13. Ibid.

14. Means, "Heavy Seas Running," 233–37.

15. Smith and Powell, *The Coast Guard,* 33.

16. "Life Saving Service Appliances File, Correspondence 1877– , A–Z," Box 7, RUSCG, RG26, National Archives.

17. Smith and Powell, *The Coast Guard,* 35; T. Michael O'Brien, *Guardians of the Eighth Sea: A History of the U.S. Coast Guard on the Great Lakes* (Washington, D.C.: U.S. Government Printing Office, 1979), 42.

18. Bennett, "The Lifesavers," 59.

19. Ibid., 61.

20. Unless otherwise noted, the requirements for superintendent, keeper, and surfman are found in *Regulations for the Government of the Life-Saving Service of the United States, January 1873* (Washington, D.C.: U.S. Government Printing Office, 1873); *Revised Regulations for the Government of the Life-Saving Service of the United States and the Laws Upon Which They Are Based* (Washington, D.C.: U.S. Government Printing Office, 1884); *Regulations for the Government of the Life-Saving Service of the United States, 1899* (Washington, D.C.: U.S. Government Printing Office, 1899).

21. Photocopy, "Memorandum for the Secretary," 20 January 1912, located in the Life-Saving Service Box, Historian of the U.S. Coast Guard, U.S. Coast Guard Headquarters, Washington, D.C. (USCG historian.)

22. O'Brien, *Guardians of the Eighth Sea,* 37.

23. Ellice B. Gonzalez, *Storms, Ships & Surfmen: The Life-Savers of Fire Island* (New York: Eastern National Park & Monument Association, 1982), 68.

24. O'Brien, *Guardians of the Eighth Sea,* 37.

25. Unless otherwise noted, all material on Keeper Dunbar Davis's rescues is found in *ARUSLSS, 1894,* 88–91; David Stick, *Graveyard of the Atlantic: Shipwrecks of the North Carolina Coast* (Chapel Hill: University of North Carolina Press, 1952), 133–43.

26. Eugene York is the only person who has produced scholarly studies of the architects and architecture of the U.S. Life-Saving Service. Eugene V. [Wick] York, "The Architecture of the U.S. Life-Saving Service," *Log of the Mystic Seaport,* 34 (Spring 1982): 3–20; Eugene V. York, "The Architecture of the United States Life-Saving Service," Master's thesis, Boston University, 1983.

27. York, "Architecture," 4–5. The architects of the service were Paul J. Pelz, Albert J. Bibb, Albert J. Tolman, and Victor Mendleheff.

28. Material on the various classes of stations are found in W. D. O'Connor, "The United States Life-Saving Service," *Appleton's Annual Cyclopedia, 1878* (New York: D. Appleton, 1879), 759.

29. Dewey Livingston and Steven Burke, *The History of and Architecture of the Point Reyes Lifeboat Station: Drakes Bay, Point Reyes National Seashore, California* (Point Reyes, Calif.: Department of the Interior, National Park Service, 1991), 5–6.

30. Unless otherwise noted, all material on the Nome Station is found in Glenda J. Choate and Thomas D. Harrison, "Station Nome and Keeper Thomas A. Ross," Public Affairs Office, U.S. Coast Guard District 17, Juneau, Alaska.

31. Sumner I. Kimball, *Organization and Methods of the United States Life-Saving Service . . . Read Before the Committee on Life-Saving Systems and Devices, International Marine Conference, November 28, 1889* (Washington, D.C.: U.S. Government Printing Office, 1912), 8.

32. Ibid., 10; Dennis L. Noble, *Gulf Coast and Western Rivers: A Brief History of U.S. Coast Guard Operations* (Washington, D.C.: U.S. Coast Guard, 1989), 8.

33. Kimball, *Organization and Methods,* 10; Dennis L. Noble, *Legacy: The United States Life-Saving Service* (Washington, D.C.: U.S. Coast Guard, 1987), 10; *ARUSLSS, 1902,* 260.

34. Unless otherwise noted, all material on the investigation of the *M & S Henderson* and the appointment of Etheridge is found in "Nomination of Keepers," District 6, RUSCG, RG26, National Archives. Charles F. Shoemaker entered the service as a third lieutenant on 20 November 1860 and was promoted to the service's highest rank, captain commandant, in 1895. One historian of the coast guard has written that Shoemaker was one of four early officers who "earned reputations as spearheads of a drive for service betterment." Dennis L. Noble, *Historical Register U.S. Revenue Cutter Service Officers 1790–1914* (Washington, D.C.: U.S. Coast Guard, 1990), 66; Stephen H. Evans, *The United States Coast Guard 1790–1915: A Definitive History* (Annapolis: U.S. Naval Institute Press, 1949), 28.

35. Herman J. Viola, *The National Archives of the United States* (New York: H. N. Abrams, 1984), 256.

36. All material on the wreck of the *Newman* is found in *ARUSLSS, 1897,* 114–15.

37. Photocopies from the Evanston (Illinois) Historical Society. For an account of the rescue see Dennis L. Noble and Truman R. Strobridge, "You Have to Go Out," *Naval History,* vol. 3 (Fall 1989): 12–20.

38. Photocopy of surfmen's pay located in the files of USCG historian.

39. Ibid.

40. Gonzalez, *Storms, Ships & Surfmen,* 87–89.

41. "Register of Employees, 1871(?)–1913(?)," RUSCG, RG26, National Archives.

42. For information on Joshua James see Sumner I. Kimball, *Joshua James—Life-Saver* (Washington, D.C.: U.S. Government Printing Office, 1909).

43. General Records of the Treasury Department, "Personnel Folders of Notable Employees, 1822–1940," Box 2, RG56, National Archives.

44. Leonard D. White, *The Republican Era: A Study in Administrative History, 1869–1901* (New York: Free Press, 1958), 10.

45. Bennett, "The Life-Savers," 55.

CHAPTER 4

1. Gonzalez, *Storms, Ships & Surfmen* is a scholarly work that is extremely useful, and J. W. Dalton, *The Life Savers of Cape Cod* (Boston: Barta Press, 1902) is a popular work.

2. "Journals," Michigan City, Indiana (27 October 1898) RUSCG, RG26, WNRC.

3. *The Wreck and Rescue of the Schooner* J. H. Hartzell, Traverse City, Mich., Brauer Productions, 1988.

4. Nell Wise Wechter, *The Mighty Midgetts of Chicamacomico* (Manto, N.C.: Times Publishing, 1974), 13.

5. A. B. Bibb, "The Life Saving Service on the Great Lakes," *Frank Leslie's Popular Monthly,* 13 (April 1882): 398.

6. Marianne Lester, "When You're Raised Around the Water, You Don't See the Danger In It," *Navy Times, Times Magazine* (17 May 1975): 13.

7. "Nomination of Keepers," District 6, RUSCG, RG26, National Archives.

8. "Register of Employees, 1871(?)–1913(?)," RUSCG, RG26, National Archives.

9. Material on Keeper Jarvis Rider is from photocopies provided by Shirley Whealton, Tuckerton, N.J.

10. Unless otherwise noted, all material on keepers is found in "Nomination of Keepers," RUSCG, RG26, National Archives.

11. Information on Theodore Roberge is from a family scrapbook and interviews with his son, Capt. T. L. Roberge, U.S. Coast Guard (Ret.), Port Angeles, Wash.

12. Information on the wreck and rescue of the *Rosecrans* is found in *ARUSLSS, 1913,* 66–74.

13. All information on surfmen along Lake Michigan is found in "Register of Employees 1871(?)–1913(?)," RUSCG, RG26, National Archives.

14. Bennett, "The Lifesavers," 63.

15. Quoted in Dennis L. Noble and T. Michael O'Brien, *Sentinels of the Rocks: From "Graveyard Coast" to National Lakeshore* (Marquette: Northern Michigan University Press, 1979), 49.

CHAPTER 5

1. *ARUSLSS, 1877,* 43.
2. *ARUSLSS, 1877,* 45; Noel T. Methley, *The Life-Boat and Its Story* (Philadelphia: J. B. Lippincott, 1912), 18.
3. Methley, *Life-Boat and Its Story,* 18.
4. Ibid., 53–55; William D. Wilkinson, "Nineteenth Century Coastal Lifeboats in the Collection of the Mariners Museum," in *Wooden Shipbuilding & Small Craft Preservation* (Washington, D.C.: Preservation Press, 1976), 55. Wilkinson's work is the best modern discussion on the subject of coastal lifeboats, and I have relied heavily on it.
5. Methley, *Life-Boat and Its Story,* 60–61.
6. Wilkinson, "Coastal Lifeboats," 55–56.
7. Ibid., 56.
8. R. B. Forbes, *Life-Boats, Projectiles, and Other Devices for Saving Life* (Boston: Parsons Lunt, 1872), 1.
9. Ibid., 2.
10. Wilkinson, "Coastal Lifeboats," 56.
11. Methley, *Life-Boat and Its Story,* 75.
12. Ibid., 76; Wilkinson, "Coastal Lifeboats," 57.
13. Wilkinson, "Coastal Lifeboats," 57.
14. Ibid.
15. Ibid.
16. Ibid.
17. Ibid., 53–54.
18. Ibid., 54.
19. William E. Ehrman, "They Had to Go Out, But the Dobbins Boat Brought Them Back," *Inland Seas: Quarterly Journal of the Great Lakes Historical Society,* 42 (Winter 1986): 238; Wilkinson, "Coastal Lifeboats," 54, 57–58.
20. *ARUSLSS, 1882,* 17.
21. *ARUSLSS, 1877,* 48.
22. Wilkinson, "Coastal Lifeboats," 59.
23. Ibid., 60.
24. Ibid., 61.
25. Ibid., 61–62.
26. Ibid., 62; for information on the Dobbins lifeboat, see Ehrman, "They Had to Go Out," 236–45.
27. Wilkinson, "Coastal Lifeboats," 62.
28. O'Connor, *Heroes of the Storm,* 268.
29. Ibid.
30. *ARUSLSS, 1887,* 162.
31. O'Connor, *Heroes of the Storm,* 273.
32. Ibid., 274–75.
33. Ibid., 275–77.
34. *ARUSLSS, 1887,* 166.
35. O'Connor, *Heroes of the Storm,* 278–79.
36. Ibid., 279.

37. Ibid.
38. *ARUSLSS, 1887,* 166.
39. O'Connor, *Heroes of the Storm,* 280; for a modern account of this rescue see Adrian L. Lonsdale, "Rescue in '86," *Inland Seas: Quarterly Journal of the Great Lakes Historical Society,* 30 (1974): 29–34.
40. Wilkinson, "Coastal Lifeboats," 62; C. H. McClellan, "The Evolution of the Lifeboat," *Marine Engineering* (January 1906): 10.
41. McLellan, "Evolution of the Lifeboat," 10–11.
42. Ibid., 10.
43. Wilkinson, "Coastal Lifeboats," 53.
44. Forbes, *Life-Boats, Projectiles, and Other Devices,* 15–17.
45. Bennett, *Surfboats, Rockets, and Carronades,* 38.
46. Peter J. Guthorn, *The Sea Bright Skiff and Other New Jersey Shore Boats* (New Brunswick, N.J.: Rutgers University Press, 1971), 80–82. For other works on surfboats see Dennis R. Means, "The Surfboat-Lifeboat *Nantasket,* Hull, Massachusetts: The Boat That 'Would Not Succeed'," *American Neptune,* 37, no. 2 (1977): 85–94; William D. Wilkinson, "Surfboat Authority Sheds Light on Race Pt. Type," *National Fisherman,* 53 (November 1972): 4B–5B.
47. Guthorn, *Sea Bright Skiff,* 80.
48. Ibid., 5.
49. Ibid., 82.
50. Ibid., 82–83.
51. Ibid., 83.
52. Ibid., 84; "Record of Boats at Lifesaving Stations, 1873–1903," RUSCG, RG26, National Archives.
53. Bennett, *Surfboats, Rockets, and Carronades,* 38.
54. Unless otherwise noted, all material concerning the wreck of the *Ephraim Williams* is located in *ARUSLSS, 1885,* 162–64. A good secondary source on the rescue is Stick, *Graveyard of the Atlantic* (Chapel Hill: University of North Carolina Press, 1952), 112–15.
55. Robert F. Bennett, *The Life-Saving Service at Sandy Hook Station, 1854–1915* (Washington, D.C.: U.S. Coast Guard, 1976), 19.
56. Methley, *Life-Boat and Its Story,* 199–200.
57. *ARUSLSS, 1891,* 17.
58. Wilkinson, "Coastal Lifeboats," 62.

CHAPTER 6

1. J. P. Barnett, *The Lifesaving Guns of David Lyle* (Plymouth, Ind.: Town & Country, 1976), 3; Forbes, *Life-Boats, Projectiles, and Other Devices,* 20–21.
2. Barnett, *Lifesaving Guns,* 5–6.
3. Bennett, *Surfboats, Rockets, and Carronades,* 44.
4. Ibid.
5. Ibid., 43–46; Barnett, *Lifesaving Guns,* 7, 9.
6. Barnett, *Lifesaving Guns,* 1–2.
7. All material concerning Lyle's experiments are found in David Alexander

Lyle, *Report on Life-Saving Ordnance and Appurtenance.* (Washington, D.C.: U.S. Government Printing Office, 1878).

8. Barnett, *Lifesaving Guns,* 1–2.

9. Kimball, *Organization and Methods,* 25–26; C. H. McClellan, *Instructions to Mariners in Case of Shipwreck . . .* (Washington, D.C.: U.S. Government Printing Office, 1908).

10. Kimball, *Organization and Methods,* 10.

11. Bennett, *Surfboats, Rockets, and Carronades,* 48–50; Rebecca Harding Davis, "Life Saving Stations," *Lippincott's Magazine,* 17 (March 1876): 310.

12. Bennett, *Surfboats, Rockets, and Carronades,* 46–53.

13. The writer took part in beach cart drills in 1959 at a U.S. Coast Guard lifeboat station on the Great Lakes.

14. "Beach Apparatus Demonstration," *Courier,* National Park Service (Summer 1978): 10.

CHAPTER 7

1. Kimball, *Organization and Methods,* 18.

2. Ibid., 19.

3. *ARUSLSS, 1876,* 11–14.

4. Methley, *Life-Boat and Its Story,* 200.

5. Quoted in Noble and O'Brien, *Sentinels of the Rocks,* 38–39.

6. Ernest H. Rankin, Sr., "Captain Henry J. Cleary Lifesaver-Showman," *Inland Seas: Quarterly Journal of the Great Lakes Historical Society,* 33 (Summer 1977): 130.

7. "Journals," Michigan City (Indiana), 20 May 1892 (Journal, Michigan City), RUSCG, RG26, WNRC; Ernest L. Osborne and Victor West, *Men of Action: A History of the U.S. Life-Saving Service on the Pacific Coast* (Brandon, Ore.: Brandon Historical Society Press, 1981), 158.

8. *ARUSLSS, 1892,* 46–48; Livingston and Burke, *History and Architecture of the Point Reyes Lifeboat Station,* 28–29.

9. Journal, Michigan City, 10 June 1897.

10. Asa Cobb Paine Lombard, Jr., *East of Cape Cod* (New Bedford, Mass.: Reynolds-DeWalt, 1976), 103–9; O'Brien, *Guardians of the Eighth Sea,* 38.

11. Kimball, *Organization and Methods,* 18.

12. Osborne and West, *Men of Action,* 153.

13. Material on the keepership of North Manitou Island is found in "Nomination of Keepers," District 11, RUSCG, RG26, National Archives.

14. Kimball, *Organization and Methods,* 17; "List of Persons Who Have Died by reason of injury received or disease contracted in the line of duty in the Life-Saving Service since the origin of the present system, as shown by the records of the Treasury Department" (Washington, D.C.: U.S. Government Printing Office, 1914[?]), 4; O'Brien, *Guardians of the Eighth Sea,* 39.

15. Kimball, *Organization and Methods,* 17–18.

16. *ARUSLSS, 1899,* 233–40. The Coston Signal was invented by Benjamin Coston, one-time chief scientist at the Washington Navy Yard. Upon his death, his widow, Martha Hunt Coston, seeking a way to support herself and four

children, found the plans and prototype of the signal. In the 1850s she took it upon herself to start a company to manufacture the device and to sell it to the U.S. Navy. Eventually, she also marketed the signal, traveling widely in Europe in this pursuit. She eventually turned over the management of the firm to one of her sons. Martha Hunt Coston died in 1902 at the age of seventy-four. Martha Coston, *A Signal Success: The Work and Travel of Mrs. Martha J. Coston, An Autobiography* (Philadelphia: J. B. Lippincott, 1886); Bernard C. Nalty, Dennis L. Noble, Truman R. Strobridge, eds., *Wrecks, Rescues, & Investigations: Selected Documents of the U.S. Coast Guard and Its Predecessors* (Wilmington, Del.: Scholarly Resources, 1978), 1–2.

17. Bibb, "Life Saving Stations on the Great Lakes," 398; quoted in O'Brien, *Guardians of the Eighth Sea*, 40.

18. Edward J. Canfield and Thomas A. Allan, *Life on a Lonely Shore: A History of the Vermillion Point Life-Saving Station* (Sault Ste. Marie, Ont.: Lake Superior State University Press, 1991), 13.

19. Journal, Point Betsie, Michigan, 19 July 1881; Dwight Boyer, *Ghost Ships of the Great Lakes* (New York: Dodd, Mead, 1968), 172–88.

20. "Scrapbooks," 1889, RUSCG, RG26, National Archives.

21. Ibid., 1899–1900, 1902–3.

22. "Nomination of Keepers," District 6, RUSCG, RG26, National Archives; "Nomination of Keepers," District 11, RUSCG, RG26, National Archives.

23. Log, Gull Shoal, North Carolina, 18 August 1899, RUSCG, RG26, WNRC. Unless otherwise noted, all material on Midgett's rescue is found in *ARUSLSS, 1900,* 25–28; "Scrapbooks," 1899–1900; Stick, *Graveyard of the Atlantic,* 166–68.

24. Information on the beach patrol just prior to and after World War II is found in Malcolm F. Willoughby, *The U.S. Coast Guard in World War II* (Annapolis: U.S. Naval Institute Press, 1957), 45–53.

25. Journal, Michigan City, Indiana, 28 July, 26 November 1890; "Scrapbooks 1874–1937"; Smith and Powell, *The Coast Guard,* 35.

26. Quoted in Julius F. Wolff, Jr., "A Lake Superior Lifesaver Reminisces," *Inland Seas: Quarterly Journal of the Great Lakes Historical Society,* 24 (Summer 1968): 109–10.

27. *ARUSLSS, 1885,* 31; Bibb, "Life Saving Service on the Great Lakes," 398.

28. Journal, Michigan City, Indiana, 2 July, 3 July, 29 July, 17 October, 19 October, 29 October 1899.

29. Lombard, *East of Cape Cod,* 151.

30. Quoted in Gonzalez, *Storms, Ships and Surfmen,* 49; "Nomination of Keepers," District 6, RUSCG, RG26, National Archives.

31. Ibid., District 4.

32. "Scrapbooks," 1900.

33. Osborne and West, *Men of Action,* 158.

34. Canfield and Allan, *Life on a Lonely Shore,* 7.

35. "Scrapbooks," 1903–4.

36. "Nomination of Keepers," District 11, RUSCG, RG26, National Archives; photocopied material from the Jesse Besser Museum, Alpena, Mich.; Gonzalez, *Storms, Ships & Surfmen,* 48–49.

37. Canfield and Allan, *Life on a Lonely Shore,* 37.

38. Wolf, "Lake Superior Lifesaver Reminisces," 113.

39. "Scrapbooks," 1902–3; "The Life Saving Station," photocopy in USCG historian's file.

40. All material on Edith Morgan's work is found in *ARUSLSS, 1880,* 39–40.

CHAPTER 8

1. Holland, *America's Lighthouses,* 32.
2. Ibid., 32, 37.
3. *ARUSLSS, 1910,* 17.
4. Evans, *United States Coast Guard,* 187–88.
5. Bennett, "The Life-Savers," 63.
6. Quoted in Evans, *United States Coast Guard,* 206.
7. Ibid., 207.
8. Evans's work and Robert Erwin Johnson, *Guardians of the Sea: History of The United States Coast Guard, 1915 to the Present* (Annapolis, Md.: Naval Institute Press, 1987) are the best works tracing the evolution of the U.S. Coast Guard.
9. All material on the merging of the U.S. Life-Saving Service and the USRCS is found in 62d Cong. 2d Sess. House Doc. 670. Economy and Efficiency in the Government Service. Message of the President of the United States Transmitting Reports of the Commission on Economy and Efficiency, 4 April 1912, 378–89, 396–97, and passim; Evans, *United States Coast Guard,* 211–15.
10. Evans, *United States Coast Guard,* 215.
11. Johnson, *Guardians of the Sea,* 32.

Selected Bibliography

The two best sources to obtain information on the U.S. Life-Saving Service are the National Archives and the annual reports of the service. The journals (logbooks) of the individual stations, currently located in the Washington National Records Center in Suitland, Maryland, are a third source of excellent information. In a decision that will make research more difficult for anyone studying the service as a national entity, the National Archives has decided to move the various logbooks to the regional record centers where the original stations were located. This decision will cause researchers the loss of a central location to obtain information on the service, that is, the Washington, D.C., metropolitan area.

ARCHIVAL SOURCES

Cartographic and Architectural Archives, Alexandria, Virginia.

Records of the U.S. Coast Guard. Record Group 26.

"Engineering Drawings"

General Records of the Department of the Treasury. Record Group 56.

"Personnel Folders of Notable Treasury Employees, 1822–1940." National Archives, Washington, D.C.

Records of the U.S. Coast Guard. Record Group 26. National Archives, Washington, D.C.

"Circulars, 1857–1924"

"Civil Service Applications for Keepers" (various dates)

"Correspondence, 1883–1902"

"Correspondence Concerning Appliances, 1888–1911"
"Correspondence of the General Superintendent, 1892–1914"
"Correspondence with Lifesaving Station Keepers, 1870–78"
"Letters Received, 1847–1914"
"Letters Sent by the Fifth, Sixth, Seventh, Eighth, and Thirteenth Districts, 1885–1902"
"Letters Sent to the Commandant, 1873–1915"
"Life Saving Service Appliances File, 1877– "
"Miscellaneous, 1849–75"
"Miscellaneous Correspondence, 1874–97"
"Miscellaneous Letters Sent to the Commandant Concerning the Life-Saving Service, 1848–56"
"Miscellaneous Letters Sent to the Commandant Concerning the Life-Saving Service, 1873–97"
"Nomination of Keepers" (various districts and dates)
"Record of Boats at Lifesaving Stations, 1873–1902"
"Register of Employees, 1871(?)–1913(?)"
"Reports of the Board of Life-Saving Appliances, 1906"
"Scrapbooks, 1874–1937"
"Semi-Official Letters Received, 1886–1910"
"Wreck Reports of Stations, 1854–1909"

Records of the U.S. Coast Guard. Record Group 26. Washington National Records Center, Suitland, Md.
"Journals of the U.S. Life-Saving Service" (various stations and dates)

BOOKS AND ARTICLES

Annual Report of the Operations of the United States Life-Saving Service, 1875–1914. Washington, D.C.: U.S. Government Printing Office.

Barnett, J. P. *The Lifesaving Guns of David Lyle.* Plymouth, Ind.: Town & Country, 1976.

"Beach Apparatus Demonstration." *Courier.* National Park Service (Summer 1978).

Bennett, Robert F. "The Lifesavers: 'For Those in Peril on the Sea'." The U.S. Naval Institute. *Proceedings* 102 (March 1976): 54–63.

———. *The Life-Saving Service at Sandy Hook Station: 1854–1915.* Washington, D.C.: U.S. Coast Guard, 1976.

———. *Surfboats, Rockets, and Carronades.* Washington, D.C.: U.S. Government Printing Office, 1976.

Benson, Rodney J. "Romance and Story of Pea Island." *U.S. Coast Guard Magazine* 6 (November 1932): 52.

Bibb, A. B. "The Life-Saving Service on the Great Lakes." *Frank Leslie's Popular Monthly* 13 (April 1882): 368–98.

Boyer, Dwight. *Ghost Ships of the Great Lakes.* New York: Dodd, Mead, 1968.

Canfield, Edward J., and Thomas A. Allan. *Life on a Lonely Shore: A History of the Vermillion Point Life-Saving Station.* Sault Ste. Marie, Ont.: Lake Superior State University Press, 1991.

Chapelle, Howard L. *American Small Sailing Craft: Their Design, Development, and Construction.* New York: W. W. Norton, 1951.

Choate, Glenda J., and Thomas D. Harrison. "Station Nome and Keeper Thomas A. Ross." Public Affairs Office, U.S. Coast Guard District 17, Juneau, Alaska. Typescript.

Clark, E. P. "Life Saving Service." *Nation,* 7 September 1899, 182.

Coston, Martha. *A Signal Success: The Work and Travel of Mrs. Martha J. Coston, An Autobiography.* Philadelphia: J. B. Lippincott, 1886.

Cox, Samuel Sullivan. *Life: Its Perils and Salvation: Speech . . . Delivered in United States House of Representatives, Tuesday, June 4, 1878. . . .* Washington, D.C.: Polkinhorn, 1878.

———. "Life Saving Service." *North American Review* 132 (May 1881): 482.

Dalton, J. W. *The Life Savers of Cape Cod.* Boston: Barta Press, 1902.

Davis, Rebecca Harding. "Life Saving Stations." *Lippincott's Magazine* 17 (March 1876): 301–10.

Dobbins, David Porter. *The Dobbins Life-Boat Illustrated.* New York: Art-Printing Works of Matthews, Northrop, 1886.

Doughty, Francis Albert. "Life at a Life Saving Station." *Catholic World* 65 (July 1897): 514–27.

Dunbar, Gary S. *Historical Geography of the North Carolina Outer Banks.* Baton Rouge: Louisiana State University Press, 1958.

Ehrhardt, John B. *Joseph Francis 1801–1893: Shipbuilder: Father of the U.S. Life-Saving Service.* Princeton: Princeton University Press, Newcomen Society, 1950.

Ehrman, William E. "They Had to Go Out, But the Dobbins Boat Brought Them Back." *Inland Seas: Quarterly Journal of the Great Lakes Historical Society* 42 (Winter 1986): 236–45.

Emery, Edwin. *History of Sanford, Maine.* Fall River, Mass.: Privately printed, 1902.

Evans, Stephen H. *The United States Coast Guard, 1790–1915: A Definitive History.* Annapolis: U.S. Naval Institute Press, 1949.

Forbes, R. B. *Life-Boats, Projectiles, and Other Devices for Saving Life.* Boston: Parsons Lunt, 1872.

Francis' Metallic Life-Boat Company. New York: William C. Bryant, 1852.

Freeman, T. J. A. "The Life-Saving Service of the United States." *American Catholic Quarterly Review* 18 (July 1893): 650–66.

Gonzalez, Ellice B. *Storms, Ships & Surfmen: The Life-Savers of Fire Island.* New York: Eastern National Park & Monument Association, 1982.

Greene, Jerome A. *Historic Structure Report Historical Data Component: Little Kinnakeet Life-Saving and Coast Guard Station Cape Hatteras National Seashore, North Carolina.* U.S. Department of the Interior: National Park Service, 1987.

Guthorn, Peter J. *The Sea Bright Skiff and Other New Jersey Shore Boats.* New Brunswick, N.J.: Rutgers University Press, 1971.

Holland, F. Ross. *America's Lighthouses: Their Illustrated History Since 1716.* Brattleboro, Vt.: Stephen Greene Press, 1972.

Howe, M. A. DeWolfe. *The Humane Society of the Commonwealth of Massachusetts: An Historical Review, 1785–1916.* Boston: Riverside Press, 1918.

Hoyt, Mary. "House of Refuge." *Compass: A Magazine of the Sea* 45 (1975): 23–24.

Hurley, George, and Suzanne Hurley. *Shipwrecks and Rescues Along the Barrier Islands of Delaware, Maryland, and Virginia.* Norfolk, Va.: Donning, 1984.

Janett, Calvin. "Family of Heroes: Saga of Mighty Midgetts." *U.S. Coast Guard Academy Alumni Association Bulletin* 31 (May–June 1969): 13–19.

Johnson, Robert Erwin. *Guardians of the Sea: History of the United States Coast Guard, 1915 to the Present.* Annapolis: Naval Institute Press, 1987.

Kaplan, H. R., and Adrian L. Lonsdale. *Voyager, Beware.* Chicago: Rand McNally, 1966.

Kimball, Sumner I. *Joshua James—Life-Saver.* Washington, D.C.: U.S. Government Printing Office, 1909.

———. *Organization and Methods of the United States Life-Saving Service. . . . Read before the Committee on Life-Saving Systems and Devices, International Marine Conference, November 22, 1889.* Washington, D.C.: U.S. Government Printing Office, 1912.

Lamb, M. J. "The American Life Saving Service." *Harper's New Monthly Magazine* 44 (February 1882): 357–73.

Lester, Marianne. "When You're Raised Around the Water, You Don't See the Danger In It." *Navy Times, Times Magazine,* 17 May 1975.

Livingston, Dewey, and Steven Burke. *The History of and Architecture of the Point Reyes Lifeboat Station: Drake's Bay, Point Reyes National Seashore, California.* Point Reyes, Calif.: U.S. Department of the Interior, National Park Service, 1991.

Lombard, Asa Cobb Paine, Jr. *East of Cape Cod.* New Bedford, Mass.: Reynolds-DeWalt, 1976.

Lonsdale, Adrian L. "Rescue in '86." *Inland Seas: Quarterly Journal of the Great Lakes Historical Society* 28 (Summer 1972): 96–101.

Lyle, David Alexander. *Report on Life-Saving Ordnance and Appurtenance. By D. A. Lyle, Ordnance Department, U.S. Army.* Washington, D.C.: U.S. Government Printing Office, 1878.

McClellan, C. H. "The Evolution of the Lifeboat." *Marine Engineering* (January 1906): 10–11.

———. *Instructions to Mariners in Case of Shipwreck with Information Concerning the Life-Saving Stations upon the Coasts of the United States.* Washington, D.C.: U.S. Government Printing Office, 1908.

Mathews, Gerald. "Life Savers of the Pacific Coast." *Californian* 4 (July 1893): 62

Means, Dennis R. "A Heavy Sea Running: The Formation of the U.S. Life-Saving Service, 1846–1878." *Prologue: Journal of the National Archives* 19, no. 4 (Winter 1987): 222–43.

———. "The Surfboat-Lifeboat *Nantasket,* Hull, Massachusetts: The Boat that 'Would Not Succeed'." *American Neptune* 37, no. 2 (1977): 85–94.

Methley, Noel T. *The Life-Boat and Its Story.* Philadelphia: J. B. Lippincott, 1912.

Nalty, Bernard C., Dennis L. Noble, and Truman Strobridge, eds. *Wrecks, Rescues & Investigations: Selected Documents of the U.S. Coast Guard and Its Predecessors.* Wilmington, Del.: Scholarly Resources, 1978.

Nalty, Bernard C., and Truman R. Strobridge. "The Lyle Gun: A Cannon That Saved Lives." *Compass: A Magazine of the Sea* 49 (1979): 8–11.

Noble, Dennis L. *Gulf Coast and Western Rivers: A Brief History of U.S. Coast Guard Operations*. Washington, D.C.: U.S. Coast Guard, 1989.

———. *Historical Register U.S. Revenue Cutter Service Officers 1790–1914*. Washington, D.C.: U.S. Coast Guard, 1990.

———. *Legacy: The United States Life-Saving Service*. Washington, D.C.: U.S. Coast Guard, 1987.

———. "Man the Surfboat!" *Inland Seas: Quarterly Journal of the Great Lakes Historical Society* 31 (Fall 1975).

———. "The Old Life Saving Station at Michigan City, Indiana: 1889–1914." *Indiana History Bulletin* 51 (October 1974): 136–43.

———. "They Are All Gone." *Proceedings of the U.S. Naval Institute* 102 (March 1976): 92–94.

———. "Vessel Ashore." *Shipmates* 3 (Fall 1975): 36–40.

Noble, Dennis L., and T. Michael O'Brien. *Sentinels of the Rocks: From "Graveyard Coast" to National Lakeshore*. Marquette: Northern Michigan University Press, 1979.

———. "That Others Might Live: The Saga of the U.S. Coast Guard." *American History Illustrated* (June 1976).

O'Brien, T. Michael. *Guardians of the Eighth Sea: A History of the U.S. Coast Guard on the Great Lakes*. Washington, D.C.: U.S. Government Printing Office, 1979.

O'Connor, William D. *Heroes of the Storm*. Boston: Houghton, Mifflin, 1904.

———. "The United States Life-Saving Service." *Appleton's Annual Cyclopedia, 1878*. New York: D. Appleton, 1879.

Osborne, Ernest L., and Victor West. *Men of Action: A History of the U.S. Life-Saving Service on the Pacific Coast*. Brandon, Ore.: Brandon Historical Society Press, 1981.

Philadelphia Board of Trade. *Report of a Special Committee of the Philadelphia Board of Trade in Relation to the Life-Saving Stations upon the Coast*. Philadelphia: King & Baird, 1860.

Pouliot, Richard A., and Julie J. Pouliot. *Shipwrecks on the Virginia Coast and Men of the United States Life-Saving Service*. Centerville, Md.: Tidewater, 1982.

Quinn, William P. *Shipwrecks Around Cape Cod*. N.p.: Knowlton & McLeary, 1973.

Rankin, Ernest H., Sr. "Captain Henry J. Cleary, Lifesaver-Showman." *Inland Seas: Quarterly Journal of the Great Lakes Historical Society* 33 (Summer 1977).

Rattray, Jeannette Edwards. *Ship Ashore! A Record of Maritime Disasters off Montauk and Eastern Long Island, 1640–1955*. New York: Coward-McCann, 1955.

———. *Perils of the Port of New York*. New York: Dodd, Mead, 1979.

Roberts, Frank B. "Midgetts Are Giant." *Veterans of Foreign Wars Magazine* 60 (June 1973): 18–19.

Shanks, Ralph C., Jr., and Janetta Thompson Shanks. *Lighthouses and Lifeboat Stations on the Redwood Coast*. San Anselmo, Calif.: Costano Books, 1978.

Smith, Darrell Hevenor, and Fred Wilbur Powell. *The Coast Guard: Its History, Activities and Organization*. Washington, D.C.: Brookings Institution, 1929.

Stackpole, Edouard A. *Life Saving Nantucket*. Nantucket, Mass.: Stern-Majestic Press, 1972.

Stick, David. *Graveyard of the Atlantic: Shipwrecks of the North Carolina Coast.* Chapel Hill: University of North Carolina Press, 1952.

Vent, Myron H. *South Manitou Island: From Pioneer Settlement to Park*. Springfield, Va.: Goodway Press, 1973.

Wechter, Nell Wise. *The Mighty Midgetts of Chicamacomico*. Manto, N.C.: Times Publishing, 1974.

Wedgewood, T. L. "In Testimony of Heroic Deeds . . ." *U.S. Coast Guard Academy Alumni Association Bulletin* 38 (May–June 1976): 35–38.

White, Leonard D. *The Republican Era: A Study in Administrative History, 1869–1901*. New York: Free Press, 1958.

Wilkinson, William D. "American Coastal Lifeboat Development—An English Contribution." *Lifeboat* 43 (Summer 1974): 178–79.

———. "Nineteenth Century Coastal Lifeboats in the Collection of the Mariners Museum." In *Wooden Shipbuilding & Small Craft Preservation*. Washington, D.C.: Preservation Press, 1976.

———. "The Standard 36-Ft. Motor Lifeboat of the U.S. Life Saving Service—1907." *Nautical Research Journal* 11 (Summer 1960).

———. "Surfboat Authority Sheds Light on Race Pt. Type." *National Fisherman* 53 (November 1972): 4B–5B.

Willoughby, Malcolm F. *The U.S. Coast Guard in World War II*. Annapolis: U.S. Naval Institute Press, 1957.

Wolcott, Merlin D. "Great Lakes Lifesaving Service." *Inland Seas: Quarterly Journal of the Great Lakes Historical Society* 18 (Spring 1962): 14–21.

———. "Heroism at Marblehead." *Inland Seas: Quarterly Journal of the Great Lakes Historical Society* 16 (Winter 1960): 269–74.

———. "Marblehead Lifesaving Station." *Inland Seas: Quarterly Journal of the Great Lakes Historical Society* 22 (Winter 1966): 295–300.

Wolff, Julius F., Jr. "The Coast Guard Comes to Lake Superior." *Inland Seas: Quarterly Journal of the Great Lakes Historical Society* 21 (Spring 1965): 14–21.

———. "A Lake Superior Life-Saver Reminisces." *Inland Seas: Quarterly Journal of the Great Lakes Historical Society* 24 (Summer 1968): 108–17.

———. "1905 Lake Superior at Its Worst." *Inland Seas: Quarterly Journal of the Great Lakes Historical Society* 18 (Winter 1962): 273–79.

———. "One Hundred Years of Rescue: The Coast Guard on Lake Superior." *Inland Seas: Quarterly Journal of the Great Lakes Historical Society* 31 (Winter 1975): 275–85.

———. "Some Noted Shipwrecks on the Michigan Coast of Lake Superior." *Inland Seas: Quarterly Journal of the Great Lakes Historical Society* 16 (Fall 1960): 172–79.

Wreck and Rescue of the Schooner J. H. Hartzell. Traverse City, Mich. Brauer Productions, 1988.

York, Eugene V. [Wick]. "The Architecture of the United States Life-Saving Service." Master's thesis, Boston University, 1983.

York, Wick [Eugene V.]. "The Architecture of the U.S. Life-Saving Stations." *Log of the Mystic Seaport* 34 (Spring 1982): 3–20.

Index

About the Author

Dennis L. Noble served in the Coast Guard at a number of shore stations and in a variety of cutters, including the *Westwind, Northwind, Edisto,* and *Evergreen,* making two trips to the Antarctic and at least six to the Arctic. He retired from the U.S. Coast Guard as a senior chief marine science technician in 1978.

Since retirement, Noble has worked as a park ranger, U.S. Army historian, and public librarian. He has a Ph.D. in U.S. history from Purdue University.

He is the author or co-author of *Wrecks, Rescues, and Investigations; Sentinels of the Rocks; The Eagle and the Dragon: The U.S. Military in China, 1901–1937;* and *Forgotten Warriors: Combat Art from Vietnam,* and more than twenty articles.